white attitudes toward black people

angus campbell

INSTITUTE FOR SOCIAL RESEARCH
THE UNIVERSITY OF MICHIGAN
ANN ARBOR, MICHIGAN

ISR Code No. 3268

Library of Congress Catalog Card No. 74-161548

ISBN 87944-007-4

Printed by Litho Crafters

Ann Arbor, Michigan

PREFACE

The major purpose of this monograph is to make available a substantial array of data regarding racial attitudes accumulated in a series of sample surveys taken by the Survey Research Center between 1964 and 1970. The first six chapters report the findings of a study undertaken in early 1968 in 15 major cities of the United States at the request of the National Advisory Commission on Civil Disorders and supported by a grant from the Ford Foundation. Chapter VII summarizes data obtained in response to a set of identical questions asked of samples of the national population in the Fall of 1964, 1968 and 1970. The final chapter considers the implications of these findings for the future of race relations in this country. These studies were supported by grants from the Carnegie Corporation, The Ford Foundation and the National Science Foundation.

The 15 city study with which this monograph is primarily concerned was initiated by the National Advisory Commission in November 1967 and was directed by Howard Schuman. Interviews with 2,945 white and 2,814 black respondents between the ages of 16 and 69 were taken during January, February and March 1968. A preliminary report of the findings, written by Angus Campbell and Howard Schuman, was presented to the Commission in June 1968 and was published by the Government Printing Office in July 1968. The present monograph extends the report of the data gathered from the white respondents in this survey. Dr. Schuman is preparing a separate report of data from the black sample.

The three national surveys summarized in Chapter VII were developed by the Center for Political Studies of the Institute for Social Research under the direction of Warren E. Miller. These samples were drawn to represent the population of voting age in the Continental United States, with a total of 1,558 respondents in 1964, 1,536 in 1968 and 832 in 1970. These three studies were mainly concerned with an

analysis of voting in the national elections of those years and the small block of questions regarding race was included as incidental to that purpose.

The planning of the 15 city study was influenced in important ways by two major sets of studies which preceded it. The surveys carried out by Louis Harris and reported in *Newsweek* magazine in 1963 and 1965 were the first large-scale national investigations of Negro attitudes in the United States and are recognized as pioneer efforts in this area. Mr. Harris kindly furnished us additional unpublished data from these surveys. The second work from which we benefited was a series of reports from the "Los Angeles Riot Study," coordinated by Nathan E. Cohen of the University of California, Los Angeles, and written by a number of social scientists including Raymond J. Murphy and James M. Watson, R. M. Tomlinson and David O. Sears, and Richard T. Morris and Vincent Jeffries. We used questions from both the *Newsweek* and Los Angeles studies in the questionnaire of our 15 city study.

In order to carry out within a very limited time period the extensive field operations required in the study for the National Commission it was necessary for the Survey Research Center to supplement its own interviewing capacities with those of other survey research organizations. We acknowledge with gratitude the assistance given us in the conduct of the field work by the National Opinion Research Center of The University of Chicago, the Survey Research Laboratory of The University of Wisconsin, and the Institute for Survey Research of Temple University.

The development of the questionnaire for the 15 city study drew on the ideas and skills of a large number of individuals. Eve Weinberg and Paul Sheatsley of the National Opinion Research Center and Charles F. Cannell, John Scott, and Joan Scheffler of the Survey Research Center provided much valuable advice. Useful suggestions came from early discussions with Nathan Caplan, Mark Chesler, Jean Converse, Edgar Epps, Patricia Gurin, James House, Irwin Katz, Albert J. Reiss, Jr., and Peter H. Rossi. Roger Waldman, representing the National Advisory Commission, was most helpful.

The design of the samples used in the four surveys reported in the following pages was under the direction of Irene Hess and Leslie Kish of the Sampling Section of the Survey Research Center. A statement regarding sample design and sampling error is given in Appendix B. Coding of the interviews was under the direction of Joan Scheffler. Computing operations at the Institute for Social Research have been under the direction of John Sonquist and Duane Thomas. Karen L. Dickinson, Paula

Pelletier, Edward Schneider, and Barbara Thomas were responsible for much of the computer processing.

Research assistance to the 15 city study was provided by Barry Gruenberg, Carolyn Jenne, Vernon Moore, and Joyce Puzzuloli at a senior level and by Kendra Head, Lisa Rubens, and Carl Smith at a junior level. Betty Jennings administered the secretarial aspects of the study and much of the typing was carried out by Susan Hudson. William V. Haney, Institute Editor, Lee Behnke, and Joyce Kornbluh helped prepare the present document for publication.

We are pleased to acknowledge the contribution made by these individuals and by the several hundred interviewers and coders to the completion of this project. The cooperation of the several thousand respondents in the four surveys was also, of course, indispensible. None of these individuals nor any of the organizations which provided financial support is in any way responsible for the interpretations and conclusions presented in this report.

Ann Arbor, Michigan   **Angus Campbell**
August, 1971

TABLE OF CONTENTS

I

THE NATURE
OF WHITE ATTITUDES

There is no simple way to describe white attitudes toward black people. There has probably never been a time when white people in this country were of a common mind regarding the black population and it seems likely that as time has gone by, what consensus there may have been in the early days of the Republic has gradually dissipated. When Negroes were a race apart, enslaved, illiterate, and brutalized, it may have been possible for whites to hold a more or less common image of them, but as black people have acquired every aspect of the heterogeneity of the majority race it has become increasingly difficult to see them as all alike.

This is not to say that we do not find white people who have a stereotyped picture of Negroes. There are many white people who hold simple "pictures in the mind" not only as regards Negroes but in reference to many other national and religious groups. They are not always negative or hostile; attitudes which are supportive of black people may be equally generalized. Everyone imposes some system of simplification on the world around him; some go further than others.

Perhaps the most immediate way to illustrate the contrast in attitudes which exists among white people in their thinking about Negroes is to reproduce excerpts from two interviews taken from the extremes of our sample of the white population of 15 American cities. The first of these was with a single man of 31 years, son of a North Carolina tobacco sharecropper, two years of college, now working as a traveling salesman in California.

What do you think was the main cause of these disturbances?
*"Nigger agitators. Martin Luther King and Rap Brown
and that black bastard Carmichael."*

Have the disturbances helped or hurt the cause of Negro
rights?
*"Hurt. Whites are starting to wise up what a danger these
people can be. They are going to be tough from now on.
People are fed up with giving in and giving them everything their little black hearts want."*

What do you think the city government could do to keep
a disturbance from breaking out here?
*"Ship them all back to Africa. Lock up all the agitators
and show them we mean business."*

Would you go along with a program of spending more
money for jobs, schooling and housing for Negroes . . .
or would you oppose it?
*"I'd oppose it. They're getting too much already. If
they want something they can damn well work for it.
The government would just waste the money anyway."*

What is it about Negroes that makes them have worse
jobs, education and housing?
"They're lazy and stupid."

Would you say that white people have a right to keep
Negroes out of their neighborhoods if they want to or
that Negroes have a right to live wherever they can afford?
*"Negroes don't have a right to live wherever they want.
They would always try to be in with the whites even
though they'd be a lot happier by themselves. I'm not
against Negroes, mind you, they should have decent
housing, good housing as they can afford, just as good
as white houses if they can pay for it, but they just
shouldn't be in white neighborhoods. It's not fair to
either side and would just cause trouble.*

*Whites can make it clear Negroes aren't welcome in the
neighborhood. They can make the climate unfriendly
and see to it that no one sells to a Negro family. They
run down property, make a mess and lots of noise and*

commotion. The real estate value goes down. Nobody in their right mind would have them in the neighborhood."

That finished the interview. Is there anything you would like to add to any of the subjects we've discussed?
"I just want to say that I don't have anything against Negroes as long as they don't get pushy and stay in their place. One of my best buddies is a nigger so I don't have anything against them."

Despite his black "buddy" and his other protestations this man stands far at the negative extreme in his attitudes toward black people. He appears to have little in common with the young woman college graduate in Philadelphia from whose interview the following excerpts were taken.

What do you think was the main cause of these disturbances?
"Dissatisfaction. They are dissatisfied with the way they live, the way they are treated and their place in the social structure of America."

Have the disturbances helped or hurt the cause of Negro rights?
"They have helped because they have forced white people to pay attention and have brought the subject out into the open and you can't ignore it anymore. They haven't helped yet but overall it will help. It caused the thinking non-Negro population of America to realize that it is really as bad as they say or that it is rumored to be and made them also more willing in a backhanded way to accept their problem and try to be willing to do something about it."

What do you think the city government could do to help a disturbance from breaking out here?
"Not only promise but actually improve conditions, education, housing, jobs, and social treatment to such a point that something is actually physically there to show them that the city government realizes their problem and is actually doing something concrete about it. Something concrete has to be in evidence to every Negro in

the city so that they feel that the city government is sincere in its efforts and therefore there is no reason to start a riot because the city is doing something to help them. Give them more opportunities, make opportunities more evident, real opportunities."

These excerpts represent only a small number of the questions which we asked of our white respondents. Because we knew from earlier studies that racial attitudes are often complicated and sometimes contradictory, we attempted in our interviews to gather as wide a range of information about perceptions, attitudes, and experiences as our research objectives required and as our time limitations permitted. We will undertake in this chapter to demonstrate the diversity of these individual reports and to examine the ways in which the various kinds of attitudes expressed relate to each other.

The interviews we have quoted give some feeling of the contrasts which exist between individuals within the white population. In order to give an overall sense of the general contours of the attitudes of our total sample we list below a selection of specific data from our numerous tables. For example, we find that of the white people living in the 15 cities of our study:

86% say they would not mind at all having a qualified Negro as a supervisor on their job,

69% think Negroes are justified in using orderly marches to protest against racial discrimination,

68% say they believe many or some Negroes miss out on good housing because white owners won't rent or sell to them,

67% say they favor laws to prevent discrimination against Negroes in job hiring and promotion, and

49% say they would not mind at all if a Negro family with the same income and education moved next door.

These proportions of the urban white population express attitudes or beliefs which might be classified as favorable to the Negro. They are offset by white opinions which are generally unfavorable:

67% say Negroes are pushing too fast for what they want,

56% believe that Negro disadvantages in jobs, education, and housing are due mainly to Negroes themselves rather than to discrimination,

51% oppose laws to prevent racial discrimination in housing,

33% say that if they had small children they would rather
they have only white friends, and
24% of those old enough to vote say they would not vote
for a qualified Negro of their own party preference
who was running for mayor.

From these data and others to be presented in the following pages, the general distribution of white attitudes may be discerned, and it is apparent that they are neither as equalitarian or as vindictively racist as they are sometimes represented to be. Extreme individuals we certainly find, including those we have quoted, but the mainstream of white attitudes is generally more moderate. White people in the cities do not talk about genocide and they do not espouse mass intermarriage. When interviewed they reveal a compromise of beliefs and opinions, some of them leaning toward the segregationist, unsympathetic, censorious side of the balance, others toward the integrationist, supportive, understanding side.

The 15 city study grew out of the violent events in Detroit and Newark and other American cities in the Summer of 1967, and was specifically intended to provide a documentation of white and black attitudes which would increase understanding of these violent episodes. This orientation focused our inquiry on the more immediate aspects of racial problems in the cities and diminished our concern with some of the broader attitudes of racial attitudes which have been the primary interest of earlier research. We have not, for example, attempted to construct the typical image white and black people have of each other; we have not undertaken to relate racial attitudes with attitudes toward other minorities; we have not explored the childhood experiences of our respondents to expose early family influences which might be responsible for adult beliefs. These would all have been valuable additions to our study, but they were precluded by the necessity of concentrating on the specific problem of the present racial confrontation in the major cities.

Scholarship in the field of race relations has distinguished between three separate components of intergroup attitudes, identified as conative, cognitive, and affective. Harding[1] describes these components in the following terms:

The *conative* components of an ethnic attitude include
beliefs about "what should be done" with regard to the

---

[1]Harding, J., Proshansky, H., Kutner, B., and Chein, I., "Prejudice and Ethnic Relations," in G. Lindzey and E. Aronson (Eds.). *Handbook of Social Psychology, Vol. V* (2nd ed.). Reading, Mass.: Addison-Wesley, 1969, 37-76.

group in question and action orientations of the individual
toward specific members of the group;

The *cognitive* components are the perceptions, beliefs,
and expectations that the individual holds with regard
to various ethnic groups;

The *affective* components of an ethnic attitude include
both the general favorability or unfavorability of the
attitude and the specific feelings that give the attitude
its affective coloring. On the positive side they include
such feelings as admiration, sympathy, and "closeness"
or identification; on the negative side they include con-
tempt, fear, envy, and "distance" or alienation.

These three components are represented in the three major measures
of interracial attitudes with which this chapter is primarily concerned. We
undertook in our questionnaire to develop sets of questions which would
tap three specific dimensions of the general orientation white people in
the cities have toward the immediate racial situation. The first of these,
conative in quality, has to do with what has historically been called
"social distance," the attitude of the white person toward personal contact of one form or another with black people.[2] The second is a cognitive measure, an assessment of the extent to which the white person per-
ceives that black people are discriminated against in various ways by white
society. The third dimension is primarily affective and relates directly to
the events which gave rise to this study; it is concerned with white sympathy with the demonstrations, sit-ins, and street rioting which we will
identify collectively as black protest.

In order to demonstrate the full range of our information about
white attitudes without creating an overwhelming confusion of detail,
we will organize the individual questions from our interview schedule
into clusters which represent the three attitude dimensions we have identified and from each cluster we will derive a scale. The interrelations of the
items which make up each scale are given in Appendix C.

Attitudes Toward Interracial Contact

Certainly no aspect of the interracial problem in this country has
been more visible or stirred more passion than that of segregation. Federal

---

[2]Bogardus, E. S., "Social Distance and its Origin," *Journal of Applied Sociology,* 9, 1925, 216-226.

and local statutes have wiped out most of the more obvious forms of physical separation of the races, such as the separate facilities which used to be commonplace, but the fact of social separation remains. Although people in the large cities see people of the other race every day, on the street, on the job, in the shops and restaurants, it is easily possible for them to go from week to week without exchanging a word across race lines. Some deliberately avoid such contact, others are indifferent about it, some seek it out.

It is one of the readily observable facts about American life that interracial contact occurs more easily under some social circumstances than others. For this reason our inquiry sought to assess white attitudes toward various forms of contact with black people, at work, in the neighborhood, through their children, and as personal friends. Table I-1 shows us how proposals of these different kinds of relationships are responded to by white people.

This brief series of questions tells us what many studies have shown before this one—that white reaction to proposals of interracial contact is a function of the degree of social distance implied. The work situation is apparently not threatening to most white people, perhaps because it involves only the more public aspects of the personality. Perhaps the current social norms for equal treatment in public relationships makes this type of association easier. In any case, people who are very resistant to other forms of contact with Negroes are very forthright in their professions of equalitarian attitudes regarding relationships on the job. Doubts begin to increase when black playmates for their children are proposed, although here again two out of three white urbanites seem undisturbed by this prospect. To many of these people this question probably implied contact at school, another semipublic area of life. We know from other research that the Supreme Court decision integrating the public schools is approved by a majority of the American population but the prospect of sending one's own child to school with more than token numbers of black children gives many white parents pause.[3]

The question of neighborhood integration divides the white urban population almost in half. This issue is confused by the economic considerations it raises in the minds of many white homeowners, but it clearly implies a closer social relationship than that associated with the job or school situation. The description of the hypothetical Negro neighbor as having similar income and education undoubtedly raised the proportion

---

[3]Schwartz, Mildred A., *Trends in White Attitudes Toward Negroes.* Chicago: National Opinion Research Center, 1967.

TABLE I-1

White Attitudes Toward Interracial Contact

	Mind a lot	Mind a little	Mind not at all		Don't know	TOTAL
"Suppose you had a job where your supervisor was a qualified Negro. Would you mind that a lot, a little, or not at all?	4%	8	86		2	100%

	Only white friends	Negro friends too		Don't care one way or other	Don't know	TOTAL
"If you had small children, would you rather they had only white friends, or would you like them to have Negro friends too, or wouldn't you care one way or the other?	33%	19		46	2	100%

	Mind a lot	Mind a little	Mind not at all	Already Negro family next door	Don't know	TOTAL
"If a Negro family with about the same income and education as you moved next door to you, would you mind it a lot, a little, or not at all?	19%	25	49	4	3	100%

	White person	Negro person		No difference	Don't know	TOTAL
"Who do you think you could more easily become friends with, a Negro with the same education and income as you or a white person with a different education and income than you?"	49%	23		5	23	100%

who found this prospect undisturbing, and we do not take this finding as a very dependable basis of predicting what would actually happen if a black family did in fact move in. Even if 49 percent of the population could be depended upon to remain calm in the face of such an eventuality there is abundant evidence from the daily newspapers that some white people are sufficiently disturbed by this form of racial integration that they are prepared to take violent action to prevent it.

Our attempt to assess the ease with which white people might enter into a friendship relationship with a black person may have been a little too hypothetical for easy understanding, but it is clear from Table I-1 that relatively few white people feel as comfortable with the prospect of a black friend as they do with a friend from their own race, even when the class matching is to the advantage of the black person. This is consistent, of course, not only with commonsense observation, but with many research findings that close personal relations between races are difficult in American society.

These four questions gave our white respondents an opportunity to respond to a range of personal relationships, differing widely in their general acceptability. If we now combine the responses of each individual to the four questions, we will be able to differentiate the white population according to the number of kinds of interracial contact they say they are prepared to accept. As we see in Table I-2, a rather small percent are either wholly accepting of such contacts, or wholly rejecting. No doubt these percentages would have differed somewhat if we had asked different questions, but the general shape of the distribution would have been similar.

TABLE I-2

Distribution of White Population on Scale of Attitudes
Toward Interracial Contact

Scale Position		Men	Women	TOTAL
1	Accept all four proposals	6%	7%	6%
2	Accept three proposals	23	18	21
3	Accept two proposals	33	27	30
4	Accept one proposal	27	32	29
5	Accept no proposals	7	12	10
	Not ascertained	4	4	4
		100%	100%	100%

Few white people in these northern cities are altogether categorical in their response to interracial integration or segregation; most of them are integrationist up to a point, beyond that they are segregationist.

Two supplementary sets of questions from our survey give us some understanding of the experiential and perceptual background which is associated with these white attitudes toward interracial contact. The first of these is a rough measure of the extent to which white individuals do in fact have friendship relationships with black people. We asked those white respondents who lived in neighborhoods which included some Negro families whether they knew any of them. Since 55 percent of our white families reported living in exclusively white neighborhoods, this left only 45 percent who might have known Negro neighbors and of these 15 percent actually did. We also asked if they had ever known Negroes outside their neighborhood with whom they were friends, and 63 percent said that they had. This is certainly a very minimal report on the amount and character of the personal contact with Negroes these people had experienced, but it may be sufficient to test the often-voiced hypothesis that resistance to integration is strongest among those white people who have had no close personal contact with Negroes. The evidence does indeed conform to expectation (r=.32)—those white people who report having Negro acquaintances in their neighborhood and Negro friends elsewhere are most likely to favor the various proposals which make up our interracial contact scale.

Although this relationship is sizable, it is apparent that many white people have attitudes toward racial integration which have no relation to their own interracial contacts. It is particularly impressive that a substantial number of those people who claim to have had Negro friends respond negatively to our proposals of various forms of contact with Negroes. Assuming these friendships to be real, they seem to be regarded by these people as purely idiosyncratic, having no relevance to the larger issue of interracial contact.

Our survey data do not permit us to impute any cause-and-effect direction in this relationship. Various experimental studies have demonstrated that under some circumstances interracial contact tends to reduce segregationist attitudes among white people.[4] In our case we do not know whether contact across racial lines produces a more generalized acceptance of interracial contact of all kinds or whether the people who told us they had black friends had those friends because their basic attitudes made it easy for them to form such associations. Probably both phenomena

---

[4]These are well summarized in Harding, J. *et al., op. cit.*

occur.   In any event, it is clear that among the forces that determine white people's attitudes toward racial integration, friendly contact with a black person may have important influence in individual cases, but it leaves unexplained a great deal of variation in the attitudes we find within the white population.

As a second effort to expand our understanding of white attitudes toward interracial contact, we undertook to ascertain the amount of cross-racial hostility our respondents felt existed. We asked these people about white dislike of Negroes: *"Do you think that only a few white people in* (CITY) *dislike Negroes, many dislike Negroes, or almost all dislike Negroes?"* And we also asked the question in reverse: *"Do you think only a few Negroes dislike white people, many dislike white people, or almost all dislike white people?"*   It is immediately apparent that the answers to these two questions are interrelated (r=.51). White people who see dislike on one side of the racial boundary are very likely also to see it on the other.

Of those whites who think almost all white people dislike Negroes:	67% believe almost all Negroes dislike whites;
	8% believe few Negroes dislike whites.
Of those whites who think few white people dislike Negroes:	53% believe few Negroes dislike whites;
	8% believe almost all Negroes dislike whites.

Is this readiness to see hostility between the races a part of a general orientation toward interracial contact? Is the tendency to see hostility in others a displacement of one's own hostility? Are those white people who see most members of both races disliking the other less ready to accept personal contact with black people? Of these questions we have a sure answer only to the last; people who see widespread hostility in others are very resistant to interracial contact themselves.

This association of perception and attitude is not as striking among those people who see relatively little conflict; they are scarcely more likely to place themselves at the favorable end of the scale than the rest of the white population. Overall the relationship between perception and attitude is rather modest (r = -.19). It would appear that those who do not see the racial picture as fraught with hostility form their attitudes regarding the acceptability of racial contacts on the basis of other considerations. But those who see themselves surrounded by hostility are for the most part unable to accept the prospect of close interracial contact. Perhaps they are motivated by a basic dislike of black people, which is expressed in both their perception of hostility and their rejection of contact. We are unable to unravel this tangled thread at this point, but we will return to the question of perceived hostility later in this volume.

Perception of Racial Discrimination

From this opening inquiry into the nature of white attitudes toward personal contact with black people we move now to consideration of another attitude domain. We have sketched the range of feeling white people in the cities have regarding various forms of racial contact and we have shown the association this feeling has with the actual experience of having black friends and the perception of much or little hostility between the races. As we will see in the next few pages, it is also related to the perception of racial discrimination. White people who say they are prepared to accept various forms of contact with Negroes are more sensitive to the presence of discrimination than those who say they are not.

The pattern of racial separation which is so deeply embedded in American history is inevitably also a pattern of racial discrimination. The sordid story of how the Negro citizen has been denied equal opportunity and equal rights need not be reviewed here. Our interest is in the measure to which white people in the cities perceive discrimination to be a fact. We recognize that in large part this perception is attitudinal rather than the result of direct experience. White people who may never have witnessed an overt act of discrimination may be convinced that serious discrimination exists. Their beliefs regarding the importance of discrimination reflect their willingness to accept information about it. We assume that the interpretation they put on their various experiences and communications expresses in part a broader orientation toward the question of race.

Several questions were asked of our white respondents to assess their perception of the presence and frequency of discriminatory practices affecting black people. The range of their answers to these questions is seen in Table I-3. Most white residents of the 15 cities are prepared to admit that black people are subject to discriminatory practices. This is particularly true in the area of housing, where, as we have seen, white people are most likely to declare themselves reluctant to accept interracial contact. Discrimination is thought to be less serious in the work situation. And, white people are particularly reluctant to accept the suggestion

TABLE I-3

White Perception of Discrimination Against Negroes

	Many	Some	Only a few	None	Don't know	TOTAL
"Do you think that in (CITY) *many, some, or only a few Negroes miss out on good housing because white owners won't rent or sell to them?"*	38%	30	22	4	6	100%
"Do you think that in (CITY) *many, some, or only a few Negroes miss out on jobs and promotions because of racial discrimination?"*	22%	34	26	12	6	100%

	Definitely	Probably	Probably not so	Definitely not so	Don't know	TOTAL
"It is sometimes said that the things we have just been talking about, such as unnecessary roughness and disrespect by the police, happen more to Negroes in (CITY) *than to white people. Do you think this is definitely so, probably so, probably not so, or definitely not so?"*	9%	29	30	26	6	100%

	Mainly due to discrim- ination	Mainly due to Negroes themselves	A mixture of both		Don't know	TOTAL
"On the average, Negroes in (CITY) *have worse jobs, education, and housing than white people. Do you think this is due mainly to Negroes being discriminated against, or mainly due to something about Negroes themselves?*	19%	56	19		6	100%

that Negroes are more subject to rough treatment and disrespect at the hands of the police than they themselves are, over half of them declaring this to be probably or definitely untrue. It is unlikely that many white people have any basis in their own observation to make a judgment of this kind and it is clear that some of them find this implied reflection on the even-handedness of American justice unpalatable.

When asked directly whether they believe the disadvantaged status of urban Negroes to be the result of discrimination or to be "something about Negroes themselves," a majority choose the latter explanation. It is important to observe that very few of these people identify this "something" as an inherent racial inferiority. Surveys over the last 25 years have shown that the belief in innate racial differences which was widely accepted at an earlier time has gradually weakened until it is now held by no more than a quarter of the national white population.[5] An even smaller fraction of the urban people of our study offer genetic inferiority as an explanation of Negro disadvantage. Most commonly the "something" they have in mind is what they take to be the Negro's lack of ambition, laziness, failure to take advantage of his opportunities. Their attitude is not one of resignation at the black man's presumed inherited limitations, but of irritation and blame that he has not done more for himself. References to their own experience, or that of their family or ethnic group, are not uncommon in white responses to this question.

In order to create a single measure of these four questions, we have cumulated the answers recognizing discrimination in each case and we find the distribution shown in Table I-4.

The sensitivity to racial discrimination which these questions tap is clearly not the same attitude as that expressed in reactions to proposed racial contact. The two measures are related (r=.24) but there are a good many people whose attitude toward interracial contact is not associated with the degree of sensitivity to discrimination one might have anticipated. One can become a strong "integrationist" without a strong feeling that Negroes are discriminated against. The fact that these two scales are to a large extent measuring different aspects of white orientation toward race is further demonstrated when we relate perception of discrimination to the individual's own extent of contact with Negroes or his perception of the extent of interracial dislike. In neither case is the relationship significant, a clear contrast to the positive relationships we saw between these measures and attitudes toward interracial contact.

---

[5]Schwartz, Mildred A., *op. cit.* See also Cohen, Nathan (Ed.), *The Los Angeles Riots.* New York: Praeger, 1970, 510.

TABLE I-4

Distribution of White Population on Scale of Perception
of Racial Discrimination

Scale Position		Men	Women	TOTAL
1	Positive response to all four questions	8%	10	9%
2	Positive response to three quesions	22	20	21
3	Positive response to two questions	28	28	28
4	Positive response to one question	22	21	21
5	Positive response to no questions	15	16	16
	Don't know	5	5	5
		100%	100%	100%

Sympathy with the Black Protest

The third measure of white attitudes which we are able to draw out of our interviews differs from the preceding two in asking for a reaction to immediately preceding events. We think it likely that in placing themselves on our measures of attitudes toward interracial contact and perception of discrimination our white respondents were expressing points of view which they had acquired over their lifetime and which do not change dramatically in response to contemporary events. In this sense they may be thought of as antecedent to the attitudes expressed by these people in reacting to the various aspects of the Negro protest.

When black violence broke out in the streets during the 1960's white people responded to the new situation from the background of their accumulated beliefs, attitudes, and values. Some joined in demonstrations of support of Negro rights; some organized vigilante groups to protect white neighborhoods. Some bought firearms, moved to the suburbs, voted for "law and order" candidates. Others "kept their cool," but it is unlikely that many white people in the cities were indifferent to the events and the rhetoric of the times.

Our study followed within a few months the violent Summer of 1967 and our questions sought to reveal white attitudes toward the activities of black people during that period. As Table I-5 demonstrates, while most white residents of the cities accept the right of Negroes to protest

TABLE I-5

White Sympathy with the Black Protest

	Are different	Are not different		Don't know	TOTAL
"Some Negro leaders are talking about having non-violent marches and demonstrations in several cities in 1968. Do you think such demonstrations are different from the riots, or that there is no real difference?"	60%	35		5	100%

	Marches and sit-ins both justified	Marches justified but not sit-ins	Neither marches nor sit-ins justified	Don't know	TOTAL
"Do you think Negroes are justified in using orderly marches to protest against racial discrimination?" IF YES: If that doesn't help, do you think Negroes are justified in protesting through sit-ins?"	28%	39	27	6	100%

	Mainly protest	Mainly looting	Some of both	Don't know	TOTAL
"Some people say these disturbances (in Detroit and Newark) are mainly a protest against unfair conditions. Others say they are mainly a way of looting and things like that. Which of these seems more correct to you?"	44%	28	24	4	100%

	Planned in advance	Some planning	Not planned at all	Don't know	TOTAL
"Do you think the large disturbances like those in Detroit and Newark were planned in advance, or that there was some planning but not much, or weren't they planned at all?	48%	36	11	5	100%

	Too fast	Too slowly	About right speed	Don't know	TOTAL
"Some say that Negroes have been pushing too fast for what they want. Others feel they haven't pushed fast enough. How about you—do you think Negroes are trying to push too fast, are going too slowly, or are moving at about the right speed?"	67%	7	22	4	100%

in an orderly way against racial discrimination, they also believe that in the urban disturbances black people have gone too far and too fast. The negative response of the white population to the disturbances and violence in the cities is seen in their answers to the questions in Table I-5. Very few white people in these cities (11 percent) thought the riots were not planned in advance at least in some degree; half of them (52 percent) felt the riots were mainly or in part a way of looting rather than primarily a protest against unfair conditions; two-thirds (66 percent) believed that sit-ins were an unjustified method of protest. In all of these cases, of course, there was a minority who expressed sympathetic attitudes and there was even a very supportive three percent who asserted that Negroes were justified in rioting if their other forms of protest were unavailing. In general the white population in these cities was accepting of the principle of peaceful demonstrations but it was repelled by the violent events which had taken place the previous summer.

These reactions to various aspects of the black protest movement relate to each other in the expected manner and in Table I-6 we bring them together in a single expression of degree of sympathy for black protest.

The fact that a sympathetic attitude toward the black protest movement is intimately bound into a broader orientation toward the whole question of white-black relationships becomes apparent when we compare this measure of sympathy to the other measures we have considered earlier. We find that far more of those white people who favored all of our proposals for interracial contact support the Negro protest than do people who resisted such contact and the overall relationship of the two measures is quite significant (r=.38). An even stronger relationship (r=.46) emerges when we compare the attitudes toward the Negro protest of white people who differ in their perception of racial discrimination. We cannot say that sensitivity to discrimination is a necessary condition for support of the black protest, but we find very little sympathy for this protest among those who are most disparaging of the presence of racial discrimination.

TABLE I-6

Distribution of White Population on Scale of Sympathy
for Black Protest

Scale Position		Men	Women	TOTAL
1	Sympathetic response to all five questions	5%	6%	6%
2	Sympathetic response to four questions	13	11	12
3	Sympathetic response to three questions	19	20	20
4	Sympathetic response to two questions	24	23	23
5	Sympathetic response to one question	26	26	26
6	Sympathetic response to none of the questions	13	14	13
		100%	100%	100%

We also find that sympathy with the black protest is associated in modest degree with both the amount of friendly contact with Negroes (r=.20) and with the perception of racial hostility (r=-.13). These relationships are not as strong as those we have just seen, but they are consistent with the general pattern of racial attitudes which has emerged in the preceding pages. People who are least sympathetic toward the various aspects of black protest are somewhat less likely to have had Negro friends and somewhat more likely to believe dislike between the races to be felt by most members of both races.

Conclusions

From this array of questions and answers we see something of the general configuration of white attitudes in the cities. It is apparent that the white population varies greatly in its feelings about race and that no "typical" person can be identified who might be said to represent the total. The safest conclusion we can draw from the distributions we have presented is that white Americans in the cities are not predominantly located at either extreme of our scales of racial attitudes. It would appear that about a fifth to a third of these people are generally positive in their racial outlook in the sense that they tend to be accepting of interracial contact, sensitive to racial discrimination, and sympathetic to various forms of black protest. A proportion of about equal size might properly be called negative, with some part of these people having very hostile attitudes indeed. In between are those numerous people whose perceptions and attitudes are ambiguous and conflicted, who are variously fair-minded, apprehensive, resentful, defensive, ill-informed, and indifferent.

The three attitude scales which we have constructed from the numerous questions asked in the interview give us three separate readings of white orientation toward race. The measure of attitudes toward interracial contact is most clearly in the tradition of research on racial attitudes. It is concerned with the question of segregation and white acceptance of more equalitarian interracial relationships. These terms have acquired a different meaning in racial rhetoric in recent years and to a black person the flavor of "tolerance" implied in these questions may seem condescending and offensive. There is little doubt, however, that for our white respondents approval of racial integration represents a more positive attitude toward black people than preference for separation. The second measure is primarily cognitive, asking the respondents how much racial discrimination they see in the world around them. We assume, of course, that these perceptions are influenced by factors other than the individual's own immediate experience with discriminatory acts and in this respect this report of perceived discrimination may be dependent on some more fundamental willingness to believe or reject information about the disadvantages of black people which we have not measured. Our third measure, sympathy with the black protest, differs from the other two in being specifically concerned with white reaction to the demonstrations and disturbances which directly preceded this study. The questions of this scale make no reference to segregation or discrimination or to any of the other traditional aspects of race relations. They are intended to assess white response to contemporary events.

Despite the fact that these three sets of questions deal with quite different content we have seen that they are not independent of each other and it is clear that there is some general factor of positive or negative orientation which runs through the three measures we have devised. We suspect that this general factor is largely affective in nature and that it is most strongly represented in our measure of reactions to the black protest. If we regard sympathy with the protest movement as the most important of the white attitudes with which this study is concerned and undertake to predict individual attitudes toward this protest from a knowledge of the other two measures, we find that both attitudes toward interracial contact and perception of discrimination contribute independently to this prediction and taken together their relationship to sympathy with the black protest is substantial (R=.54). If we look at that part of the white population whose attitudes might be expected to show the highest degree of internal structure, the college graduates, we see that the interrelations of our attitudinal measures are consistently higher than they are for the population as a whole and the combined relationship of attitudes regarding interracial contact and perception of discrimination with sympathy with the black protest becomes rather impressive (R=.66).

The three measures with which we have been concerned in this chapter were intended to represent different aspects of white attitudes toward black people and it is apparent that they do so. They have a degree of commonality, as might have been expected, but it is not so strong as to justify concluding that they are all simply measuring the same thing. Because of this degree of independence and because of the qualitative differences in the content of the three measures, we will continue to treat them separately in the ensuing pages rather than combining them into a single measure.

II

ATTITUDES
TOWARD SOCIAL ACTION

At the time the 15 city survey was conducted in early 1968 public controversy over national and local response to the problem of urban disorder was intense. In order to extend our information regarding white attitudes in this situation we undertook to assess reactions to the various policies, supportive and punitive, which were being proposed. Our interview contained four separate inquiries: the first dealt with proposals for legislative action in support of civil rights, the second with federal economic aid to the cities, the third with the use of police control by local authorities, and the fourth with counterrioting by whites. These questions were all concerned with social action in response to the pressure for racial change, by society generally, by the city government, or by individual members of the white population, and this chapter will examine white attitudes toward these actions. We will consider at the end of the chapter the findings from a single question in which we asked the respondents about any individual action they themselves might have taken in response to the racial situation. This addition will provide a very limited array of information regarding racial action by white people but it permits us to carry our analysis one further step, from racial attitudes to attitudes toward social action and finally to individual action itself.

Attitudes Toward Civil Rights Legislation

The first major effort in this century to utilize "stateways" to alter folkways in the area of race relations occurred during the Second World War when the Executive Office of the President issued its directive regarding fair employment practices in defense industries. This order was met with loud protest at the time, but the pressure for legal restraints on discrimination in hiring and promotion continued after the War and in time statutes to this effect were enacted in several states. A federal prohibition on such discrimination was written into the Civil Rights Act of 1964.[1]

Legislative support of proposals to outlaw discrimination in housing has been much more reluctant. During the 1960's, however, a number of municipalities and states enacted statutes intended to guarantee equal treatment to Negroes seeking to rent or buy housing. Although these statutes characteristically covered only a fraction of the total housing market, in some cases they went beyond the tolerance of the constituency involved and more than one of them was overturned by referendum. None of these ordinances had any remarkable effect on the actual pattern of racial housing, but the issue has acquired a certain symbolic importance and in some areas it has been the stimulus for protracted public demonstrations. Finally in 1968, having failed to do so in 1966, the Congress wrote an open housing clause into the Civil Rights Act of that year and it is now contrary to federal law, except in restricted circumstances, to deny housing to a *bona fide* applicant on the basis of his race.

Two questions were asked in our study to assess the willingness of white people to support these legislative attempts to protect the civil rights of Negroes and as we see in Table II-1, their reactions to these questions differed substantially.

Most white people in these northern cities accept without much question the rights of Negroes to equal treatment on the job and two-thirds of them believe this right should be protected by law. As we see, the number of white people who are willing to say that a white person should be given preference over a qualified black person in hiring and promotion is very small indeed. Housing, implying as it does approach to the private aspects of life, raises more doubts and half of the white population oppose statutes to guarantee open housing. Of this half, three out of five (nearly one-third of the total white population in these cities) believe that white people have a right to set up racial barriers in their neighborhoods if they choose to. As one might expect, white responses to these two proposals are closely related and we can combine their answers to form a single scale.

---

[1]The history of these events is given by Harold C. Fleming in "The Federal Executive and Civil Rights: 1961-1965," *Daedalus*, Fall 1965, 921-948.

TABLE II-1

White Attitudes Toward Civil Rights Legislation[a]

	Favor	Oppose	Believe white people should have job preference	Not ascertained	TOTAL
"Do you favor or oppose laws to prevent discrimination against Negroes in job hiring and promotion?"	67%	19	4	10	100%

	Favor	Oppose	Believe white people have right to keep Negroes out of neighborhood	Not ascertained	TOTAL
"How about laws to prevent discrimination against Negroes in hiring or renting houses and apartments? Do you favor or oppose such laws?"	40%	21	30	9	100%

[a]Both of the questions presented in this table followed a screening question which is not presented. The sequence of questions was as follows:

"In choosing people to fill jobs with higher pay and responsibility, do you think first preference should go to qualified white people, or to qualified Negroes, or that race should not make any difference one way or the other?"

(UNLESS FIRST PREFERENCE TO WHITE PEOPLE)

"Do you favor or oppose laws to prevent discrimination against Negroes in job hiring and promotion?"
"Which of these statements would you agree with:
First, white people have a right to keep Negroes out of their neighborhoods if they want to, or
Second, Negroes have a right to live wherever they can afford to just like white people?"

(UNLESS BELIEVES WHITES HAVE RIGHT TO KEEP NEGROES OUT)

"How about laws to prevent discrimination against Negroes in buying or renting houses and apartments? Do you favor or oppose such laws?"

TABLE II-2

Distribution of White Population on Scale of Attitudes
Toward Civil Rights Legislation

Scale Position		Men	Women	TOTAL
1	Favor both proposals	36%	34%	35%
2	Favor one proposal; reject other	16	13	14
3	Favor one proposal, favor discrim- ination in other	15	16	15
4	Favor discrimination or oppose legislation in both jobs and housing	19	17	18
	Not ascertained	14	20	18
		100%	100%	100%

Individual reactions to suggestions for action in the area of race should be consistent with the individual's background of racial attitudes. We expected to find that white people who are favorable toward interracial contact would also favor legislation to prevent racial discrimination and the relationship between these two measures is indeed sizable ($r=.47$). Nearly three-quarters of those white people who placed themselves at the favorable extreme of our scale of racial contact support the two legislative acts we proposed. The contrast between them and those people who were most opposed to interracial contact is substantial, although the latter are not as polarized in their feelings about civil rights legislation as the former.

Those white people who are most sensitive to discrimination against Negroes are very likely to support legislation to forbid such discrimination. However, a sizable number of white people who are least aware of discrimination also support these legislative guarantees, apparently less from a sense of present grievances as from a more abstract concept of justice. The overall relationship is not high ($r=.24$).

A similar pattern appears when we compare the acceptability of civil rights legislation to people who differ in their reactions to the black protest. Most white people who are very sympathetic to the protests of Negroes support both of the two civil rights laws proposed (82 percent). White people who feel strongly that the black protest is moving too fast and too violently are more than likely to be opposed to the ultimate objects of the protests as well but their attitudes are not as extreme as those of the people who are most supportive. The overall relationship is quite significant, however (r=.38).

We see that the approval or disapproval of civil rights legislation is more strongly related to our measure of attitudes toward interracial contact than it is to the other two. This seems intuitively reasonable since the two legislative proposals involve jobs and housing which are also areas of proposed contact. In the case of perception of discrimination and sympathy for black protest the relationship with the civil rights measure is reduced by the fact that a good many white people who are very negative on these measures still find it possible to support legislation for fair housing and employment practices. It is obviously not necessary to see widespread discrimination to feel it is desirable to have legislation to prevent it. It appears that some of the people who are most repelled by the direct action of the black movement for change are not offended by proposals for legislative action in defense of civil rights.

We do not find any substantial relationship between attitudes toward civil rights legislation with either actual personal contact with Negroes or with perception of racial hostility. People who report personal contact with black people are somewhat more likely to favor the proposed legislative acts but the tendency is not very pronounced (r=.18). The same can be said about the perception of racial hostility. White people who think the numbers of the two races who dislike each other is small are more likely to favor civil rights legislation than those who see much hostility on both sides. But the overall relationship is modest (r=-.14).

Attitudes Toward Federal Aid to Cities

The increasing complexity of the problems of the cities and the increasing intensity of conflict in the city streets has led some urban leaders to a sense of despair at the ability of city government to cope with their mounting difficulties and a demand for the federal government to intervene with massive economic support.

We were concerned in our study to assess the acceptability to the urban population of various proposals of federal aid to the cities which have come into public discussion. The four questions we asked and the distribution of answers are displayed in Table II-3.

The fact that a majority of white people in the cities give a positive answer to each one of these proposals does not come as a surprise. The role of the federal government in the solution of broad social problems has long since become an accepted fact of political life in the minds of

TABLE II-3

White Attitudes Toward Federal Aid to the Cities

	Government should do this	Government should not do this	Not ascertained	TOTAL
"Some people say that if there are not enough jobs for everyone who wants one, the government should somehow provide the extra jobs needed. Others say the government should not do this. What is your opinion?"	59%	37	4	100%
"Some neighborhoods in and around (CITY) have public schools with better buildings and more trained teachers than others. Do you think the government should provide money to bring the poorer schools up to the standard of the better schools or that the government shouldn't do this?"	78%	15	7	100%
"There are areas in cities like (CITY) where the housing is rundown and overcrowded. Some say the government should provide money to improve the housing in such places. Others don't think the government should do this. What is your opinion?	59%	36	5	100%

	Would go along with it	Would oppose it	Don't know	TOTAL
"If top government officials in Washington said that a program of spending more money for jobs, schools, and housing for Negroes is necessary to prevent riots, would you go along with such a program or would you oppose it?"	66%	28	6	100%

most Americans. Having seen the government come to the aid of the
farmers, the elderly, the veterans, the indigent, and many other special
groups and interests, the public naturally turns to it again to solve the
problems of the cities.

Adding the positive answers to the four questions into a single scale
we reveal the distributions in Table II-4.

TABLE II-4

Distribution of White Population on Attitudes
Toward Federal Aid to Cities

Scale Position		Men	Women	TOTAL
1	Favor all four proposals	31%	34%	32%
2	Favor three proposals	26	26	26
3	Favor two proposals	20	20	20
4	Favor one proposal	12	11	12
5	Favor none of the proposals	10	5	8
	Don't know	1	4	2
		100%	100%	100%

The relationship of this scale to that representing attitudes toward
civil rights legislation is clear, but it is not as sharp as one might have anticipated (r=.26). We might have expected to find a common element of
"New Deal liberalism" in these two measures and indeed we do find a
significant association. But it is apparent that the government aid questions
are touching an attitude domain which is not identical with that represented
by the civil rights issue. Perhaps this is because the civil rights questions
imply legal support for the black population while the government aid
questions imply economic support. Perhaps it is because the government
aid questions are for the most part only inferentially racial while the civil
rights questions are specifically racial. In any case, the two sets of questions
are only moderately related.

Attitudes toward federal aid relate in varying degree with the more
generalized racial attitudes, most strongly with sympathy with black protest (r=.31), less strongly with perception of discrimination (r=.24) and,
in contrast to the measure of attitudes toward civil rights legislation, least

strongly with attitudes toward interracial contact (r=.16). We learn nothing further about attitudes toward federal aid by examining their relationship to either extent of personal interracial contact or perception of racial hostility. Neither of these characteristics seems to contribute anything to the determination of how people feel about federal economic programs to aid the cities.

Attitudes Toward Police Control

The violence which broke out in the streets of Detroit and Newark in the Summer of 1967 along with the numerous other lesser acts of rioting in other cities brought the governments of the urban communities under great pressure to find a way to prevent such outbursts in the future. Some cities have responded by equipping their police with heavier weapons—and in some cases with armored vehicles—in the apparent belief that the more militant manifestations of the Negro protest could be contained by tighter police control. Others have undertaken to ameliorate the circumstances of their Negro population through programs of employment and job training, low cost housing, recruitment of Negro policemen, and similar efforts to respond to specific Negro grievances. Some, out of indecision as to the proper course, have done something of everything.

White people in the cities are confronted in their individual thinking with the same problem; do they want their city to meet the problem of riots by repressive measures, through an increase in police power, or do they believe the problem could be better met by working to improve the condition of black people in the cities. In order to ascertain the choice of the white population between these alternatives we asked two questions, the first an open-ended question referring to the immediate action their city government might take and the second a closed question asking the "best thing to do about the problem of riots" over the next five or ten years.

As we see in Table II-5, when white people in these cities are asked to propose "the most important thing" their city government can do to keep disturbances from breaking out they are more likely to think in terms of measures involving stronger police action than they are of measures intended to improve the circumstances of the Negro population. This view, held by nearly half the white population, was expressed in various ways; enlarge the police force, give police the power to shoot, arrest agitators, pass stricter laws, separate blacks from whites, and the like. Those who thought of improving Negro conditions, one-third of the total, spoke of improving the schools, providing more jobs, ending discrimination, improving housing and recreational centers, improving communication between the black community and the city leaders, and similar suggestions. There were a few who spoke of the power of prayer or of planned parenthood or who thought the problem was insoluble. One white person in eight, most of them women, simply could not offer any suggestions.

TABLE II-5

"What do you think is the most important thing the city government in (CITY) *could do to keep a disturbance like the one in Detroit from breaking out here?"*

	Men	Women	TOTAL
Stronger police control	52%	42%	47%
Improve Negro conditions	32	34	33
Other	7	7	7
Don't know	9	17	13
	100%	100%	100%

The 47 percent of the white population who feel that the most important thing to do about the problem of riots is to tighten police control are very considerably less likely to favor either civil rights legislation or federal aid to the cities than are the 33 percent who favor various measures to improve the condition of urban Negroes. This is as it should be, of course, since improving the condition of Negroes implies the kinds of legislative action these two measures propose. There is obviously a common element in reactions to these three measures.

Preferences for alternative ways of preventing riots are also substantially related to the three general racial attitudes. As we see below, those people who are most positive toward interracial contact are far less likely to recommend tighter police control than are those who are most negative. Nearly three-quarters of those who declare themselves most opposed to interracial contact propose stronger police control as the preferred method of preventing riots.

It is noteworthy that among white people most receptive to interracial contact as many as 29 percent think first of police control in answer to our question. We find similar proportions among those who stand at the positive extreme of our other two scales of racial attitudes. Apparently

TABLE II-6

Relation of Attitudes Toward Interracial Contact
to Preferred Method of Preventing Riots

	Stronger police control	Improve condition of Negroes	Other	Don't know	TOTAL
Most positive toward interracial contact	29%	60%	6%	5%	100%
Most negative toward interracial contact	71	14	8	7	100%

these people were thinking in terms of immediate action their city might take in an emergency situation. We will see when we examine the response of these people to "the best thing to do" over the next five to ten years that nearly all of this preference for police action disappears.

The preferences of those people who are most and least sensitive to the presence of racial discrimination are very similar to those who are most and least receptive to interracial contact.

TABLE II-7

Relation of Perception of Discrimination
to Preferred Method of Preventing Riots

	Stronger police control	Improve condition of Negroes	Other	Don't know	TOTAL
Most sensitive to racial discrimination	23%	63	7	7	100%
Least sensitive to racial discrimination	64%	19	5	12	100%

Finally, we see that sympathy for the black protest also predicts significantly how white people feel about ways of controlling riots. In this case two out of three of the least sympathetic people proposed tighter police control, while three out of four of the most sympathetic rejected this solution in favor of the improvement of Negro conditions.

TABLE II-8

Relation of Sympathy for the Black Protest
to Preferred Method of Preventing Riots

	Stronger police control	Improve condition of Negroes	Other	Don't know	TOTAL
Most sympathy for black protest	14%	72	8	6	100%
Least sympathy for black protest	64%	14	6	16	100%

White people who report knowing black people in their neighborhoods and elsewhere are not much more likely to reject police control as the solution to riot problems than are people who have no such cross-racial contacts. However, those people who see a great deal of "dislike" between whites and blacks are perceptibly more likely to urge more rigid police control than are those who see little. This is not the first indication we have seen, nor will it be the last, of the high incidence of negative attitudes among those white people who see the world of race characterized by mutual dislike.

TABLE II-9

Relation of Perception of Interracial Dislike
to Preferred Method of Preventing Riots

	Stronger police control	Improve condition of Negroes	Other	Don't know	TOTAL
Believe few whites and blacks dislike each other	42%	35	7	16	100%
Believe nearly all whites and blacks dislike each other	68%	15	6	11	100%

If we turn now to our second question on methods of preventing riots, couched specifically in terms of the next five to ten years, we will see that we have greatly increased the proportion of our respondents who prefer an attempt to improve the conditions of Negroes (Table II-10). Apparently the more long-term prospect makes the alternative of police action seem less appropriate to many people who had proposed stronger police control in answer to the earlier question.

TABLE II-10

"Thinking about the next five to ten years, what do you think would be the best thing to do about the problem of riots—build up tighter police control in the Negro areas, or try harder to improve the condition of the Negroes?"

	Men	Women	TOTAL
Tighter police control	18%	17%	17%
Improve Negro conditions	52	55	54
Both	28	26	27
Don't know	2	2	2
	100%	100%	100%

When we look at those people (about one-sixth of the white sample) who still regard "building up tighter police control in the Negro areas" as the best thing to do even on a five to ten year perspective we find that we have identified a segment of the white population who bulk large among those people at the negative extremes of our racial attitude scales (Table II-11). White people with a strongly positive orientation toward race almost all reject stronger police control as the best long-term solution to the problem of urban violence.

We see in the foregoing tables the remarkable extent to which those white people who stand at the extremes of our measures of racial attitudes reflect those attitudes in their preferred method of preventing riots. For most of these individuals the answer to the critical question of whether to rely on police repression or on programs intended to improve the conditions from which riots come is predictable from a knowledge of their basic racial attitudes. Of course we do not find this degree of correspondence between attitudes and preferred actions throughout the entire distribution of white

TABLE II-11

Proportion of White Respondents With Extreme Racial Attitudes Preferring
Tighter Police Control Over the Next Five to Ten Years

Most positive to interracial contact	3%	Least positive to interracial contact	31%
Most sensitive to racial discrimination	2%	Least sensitive to racial discrimination	27%
Most sympathetic to black protest	0%	Least sympathetic to black protest	30%

attitudes. Those white people whose attitudes are ambiguous and contradictory scatter their preferences for action in much less predictable ways. But those whose responses to our various questions are so consistent as to place them at the positive or negative ends of our attitude scales are also highly consistent in their responses to this choice of alternative actions.

Attitudes Toward Counterrioting

One of the impressive aspects of the urban riots during the decade of the sixties was the almost total absence of white intervention. In the first half of this century, riots involving Negroes almost invariably took the form of white aggression against blacks, with the white participants typically outnumbering the black. In the more recent period when black rioters have taken to the streets, white people have either stayed out of the area or, in isolated cases, have joined the Negroes in the looting and tumult.

There are several plausible explanations for this turn of events. It may well be that the masses of black people who were involved in the recent riots have been so large as to intimidate any response by white people. The riots have occurred within areas which are largely black and where white opposition would be at a great disadvantage. Or it is possible that police action is now more effective in cordoning off the riot area and preventing a white-black confrontation. It is also conceivable that during the postwar period there has been a significant change in white attitudes toward anti-Negro violence. The not-so-distant time when the lynching of Negroes was carried out as a public spectacle is now happily passed even in the Deep South. Violent acts remain, but public disapproval has reduced them in number and driven them underground.

Perhaps the white population of the northern cities have outgrown the day when they were ready to condone organized attacks on black people.

The only fact we can contribute to these speculations is the finding that very few white people are prepared to say that whites should respond to Negro riots by "rioting against them." As Table II-12 demonstrates, only one person in twenty specifically rejects the alternative of leaving such matters "entirely to the authorities."

TABLE II-12

"Some people say that if Negroes riot in (CITY) *next summer, maybe whites should do some rioting against them. Others say such matters should be left entirely to the authorities to handle. What do you think?"*

	Men	Women	TOTAL
Whites should do some rioting	8%	3%	5%
Should be left to the authorities	90	95	93
Don't know	2	2	2
	100%	100%	100%

We obviously do not take the answers to this question as an indication of how many white people might take to the streets in a particular situation, or how they might react if a racial conflagration got under way. No doubt under some circumstances the reliance on authority would be far less impressive than the table would suggest. We are primarily interested at this point in that small minority who are ready to condone white rioting against Negroes and to examine the background of racial attitudes which lies behind this hostile position.

Approval of counterrioting is concentrated very heavily among white people whose racial attitudes are negative. This is particularly evident among white men, among whom a disposition to violent action of this kind is considerably more common than among women. White people who are most favorably disposed toward interracial contact nearly all reject rioting as an answer to violence by black people and the same is true of those people who are most sensitive to discrimination and those most sympathetic to the black protest.

Perhaps the most striking aspect of these comparisons is the relatively limited number of those white persons most negative on racial

TABLE II-13

Relation of Attitudes Toward White Counterrioting to General Racial Attitudes

	Attitude Toward Interracial Contact				
	Favorable				Unfavorable
	1	2	3	4	5
Proportion of *total* who favor counterrioting	1	4	5	6	10
Proportion of *men* who favor counterrioting	1	5	8	8	17

	Perception of Discrimination				
	High				Low
	1	2	3	4	5
Proportion of *total* who favor counterrioting	0	5	6	6	7
Proportion of *men* who favor counterrioting	0	7	9	9	11

	Sympathy for Black Protest					
	High					Low
	1	2	3	4	5	6
Proportion of *total* who favor counterrioting	0	2	4	3	9	8
Proportion of *men* who favor counterrioting	0	4	5	6	14	10

questions who approve of violent reaction to Negro rioting. One may argue, of course, that any proportion of such people is too high, but it is apparent that it could be very much higher than it is. It would be most illuminating to know what this proportion might have been 25 or 50 years ago and what the trend in white attitudes in this regard is. As we will see later, it is not an attitude which is characteristic of the older generations. On the contrary it is strongest among the youngest groups, where, paradoxically, racial attitudes are generally more positive than they are among the older cohorts.

As we might expect, white people who condone counterrioting are found most commonly among those people whose other recommendations for social action are negative or punitive.

TABLE II-14

Relation of Attitudes Toward White Counterrioting
to Attitudes Toward Social Actions

	Total	Men
Proportion Approving Counterrioting Among Those Who:		
Oppose civil rights legislation	10%	16%
Oppose federal aid to cities	10%	12%
Favor stronger police control now	8%	13%
Favor tighter police control over the next five to ten years	13%	20%

In particular we observe that a full fifth of that part of the white male population who believe that over the next decade stronger police control is the best solution to urban riots are ready to approve rioting by white people. There may appear to be a certain contradiction in this willingness to take the law into their own hands among people who urge more intense police surveillance, but one wonders if there is not underneath these attitudes a certain taste for violence.

One further inquiry into our data produces an additional insight into this inclination toward violence among white people. A look at the individual reports of amount of personal contact with Negroes tells us nothing at all about disposition toward counterrioting. But when we divide people according to the amount of "dislike" they see between the races we find this is the most discriminating question of any of those we asked. One in four of those white men who believe "almost all" members of each race dislike the other race are prepared to justify rioting by whites. We have suggested earlier that these perceptions of dislike might in some cases be a projection of personal hostility and for these men the association of perception and attitude seems evident.

TABLE II-15

Relation of Attitudes Toward White Counterrioting
to Perception of Dislike Between Races

	High				Low
	1	2	3	4	5
Proportion of *total* approving counterrioting	16	10	5	3	1
Proportion of *men* approving counterrioting	26	13	7	5	0

Individual Action

In Table I-5 we reviewed the answers our white respondents gave to a question as to whether they thought "Negroes have been trying to push too fast for what they want." Two-thirds of them felt Negroes were indeed pushing too fast; most of the rest felt they were moving at the right speed or were in fact moving too slowly. We followed this inquiry with a secondary question asking those respondents who thought Negroes were moving too fast whether they themselves had "given money or taken part in anything that would help slow them down." Those who felt Negroes were not moving too fast were asked if they had "given money or taken part in anything that would help Negroes get what they want."

Of the 2,582 white respondents only a half dozen admitted doing anything to hinder the Negro movement for change. Two of these people had given money for various anti-integration causes, one (a realtor) had circulated a petition to recall an open housing ordinance, one felt that in paying taxes he was opposing change, one had been called up in the National Guard to patrol a disturbance area, and one angrily refused to reveal what he had done, although he admitted having done something. Most of this handful of people were quite negative toward black people; half of them approved white violence against Negroes in event of a disturbance. The only one of these people who seemed free of any negative attitude was the young National Guardsman who found himself involuntarily restricting Negro activity in his city. It appears that very few white people in these cities have actually taken any action in opposition to what Negroes are trying to achieve but those who have are likely to reveal a background of unusually hostile attitudes toward black people.

About eight percent of the white sample told us they had done something to help the Negro cause. These reports ranged from taking part in
a sit-in to giving old clothes to a Negro maid; we have clustered them into four categories as follows:

Political activism: have participated in some form of protest, e.g., sit-in, freedom march, picketing, boycott, cir-
culating petitions, voter registration.

Nonpolitical activism: have participated in some service-
type activity, e.g., Big Brother to Negro boy, Negro
Boys Club, Boy Scout or Girl Scout leader, volunteer
tutoring, providing foster home for Negro child, neighborhood visitation program.

Nonactive political support: support involves minimal
action, e.g., membership in or financial contribution to
a civil rights organization, writing letters to government
officials, signing petitions.

Nonactive nonpolitical support: support involves minimal
action, e.g., contributions to Negro College Fund or a
Negro church, gifts to someone who comes to the door,
gifts to funds which help both whites and Negroes (Community Chest), help given on individual basis to Negro
employees.

It is clear that these categories decline in the intensity of involvement in
racial questions they imply and that the final category is qualitatively
rather different from the other three. A little over one percent of the
white sample report an activity in each of the first three categories and
about four percent report an activity which falls in the fourth category.
Because the number of cases in the more active and political categories is
so small we will combine these three groups of people into one category
which we will designate "active and/or political" and compare it to the
"nonactive nonpolitical" category.

The relationship between attitudes and behavior has been the subject of much controversy among social scientists. The research evidence
is conflicting but it seems apparent that behavior is seldom fully predictable from a knowledge of attitudes alone.[2] When we examine the re-

---

[2]For a recent review of this issue see Ehrlich, H. J., "Attitudes, Behavior, and
the Intervening Variables," *American Sociologist, 4,* 1, 1969, 29-34.

lationship between the racial attitudes of our white respondents and their reports of racial actions of an active and/or political character they have taken we find a very familiar picture. Those people whose attitudes are strongly negative almost never report taking a positive action; at this extreme of the attitude scales the predictability of behavior is well-nigh perfect. Those people whose attitudes are strongly positive are far more likely to report positive action but only a minority of them do so. The evidence appears in Table II-16.

TABLE II-16

Relation of Racial Attitudes to White Reports of Positive
Racial Action
(Entry is proportion of attitudinal category reporting positive action)

Type of Action Reported	Attitude Toward Interracial Contact					
	Most positive				Most negative	
	1	2	3	4	5	
Active and/or political	22	6	2	0	0	
Nonactive, nonpolitical	6	5	4	4	3	

	Perception of Discrimination					
	Most positive				Most negative	
	1	2	3	4	5	
Active and/or political	21	3	2	1	0	
Nonactive, nonpolitical	6	5	5	2	3	

	Sympathy with Black Protest					
	Most positive					Most negative
	1	2	3	4	5	6
Active and/or political	36	7	3	*	0	0
Nonactive, nonpolitical	10	10	5	5	1	0

If we take these reports of positive action at face value we must conclude from Table II-16 that while relatively few white people take any action at all in response to the Negro pressure for change, those who do are people who stand at the extremes of the distribution of racial attitudes. The actions they report are nearly always consistent with their attitudes. However, these activists make up only a small proportion of those white people with extremely positive or negative attitudes, most of whom do not carry their racial views into any kind of overt expression. We did not ask these people who reported themselves most positive to the Negro movement why they did not translate their attitudes into action but we assume that many of them were inhibited by situational pressures of one form or another, particularly social disapproval.[3] There are also undoubtedly personality considerations which make it easier for some people to adopt a passive, detached posture rather than an active one regarding social involvement. Whatever these impediments to the implementation of good intentions may be they are obviously effective; most white people do not lend any active support to the Negro movement even when they are generally sympathetic to it.

Nevertheless, it is quite clear where the active support of the Negro cause is coming from in the white population; it comes almost entirely from that small minority whose racial attitudes are most positive. Those white people who have some doubts about social contact with black people, who do not see the facts of racial discrimination or who have mixed feelings about the Negro protest do not do anything to aid the Negro cause. It is interesting to see, however, that some of them do report various charitable acts which do not imply any threat to established racial patterns. It is apparent from Table II-16 that nonpolitical acts of this kind are reported about as frequently by people who are negative toward interracial contact and insensitive to discrimination as they are by those whose attitudes are positive in these respects. Those who are out of sympathy with the black protest, however, do not report any kind of help or support to black people.

It is regrettable that our survey was not able to explore the racial actions of white people more fully. Our limited information is sufficient, however, to demonstrate that overt actions by whites in response to the current Negro pressure for change are almost invariably based on strong attitudinal convictions, either positive or negative. On the other hand,

---

[3]Rokeach's discussion of "attitude-toward-situation" is relevant to this question. See Rokeach, M., *Beliefs, Attitudes and Values*. San Francisco: Jossey-Bass, 1968, 118.

strong attitudinal convictions are not always expressed in overt social action; more commonly than not they remain implicit, expressed perhaps in conversation or social courtesies or even in voting, but not in the kinds of activism we have been discussing.

Conclusions

Our survey has in effect submitted a series of proposals for social action to a plebiscite of the white population of the northern cities. For the most part their collective response is quite clear-cut. They certainly favor laws to prevent discrimination in hiring and promotion; they give substantial majorities to various suggested federal programs of aid to the cities. They believe that a long-term solution to the disorder problem will require more than simply building up the police force. They are almost unanimously opposed to individual white people taking the law into their own hands in case of a disturbance. Only in the case of open housing ordiances do they equivocate and here their opinions are more nearly divided.

No doubt we could have found questions which would have evoked majority disapproval, but the evidence from this survey and other studies makes it clear that the prevailing white attitude in these cities is far from the monolithic opposition to change that it is sometimes represented to be. To be sure, every extreme of opinion can be found among these people, and as usual, those people whose opinions are most extreme are most intense about them. But if we look at the totality of the white population instead of at particularly vocal individuals we see a great confusion of opinions within which there is a varying degree of readiness to change traditional racial patterns and a varying acceptance of the changes which are already occurring.

It is important to recall at this point our earlier finding of a strong inclination among the white people of these northern cities to believe that the main responsibility for action to improve the situation of black people should come from Negroes themselves. Although most of the white population has given up the belief that Negroes are inherently incapable of competing on an equal footing with whites, they have not accepted the alternative argument that Negro deficiencies are due to environmental barriers. Over half of our white respondents see the poor education, low employment status, and substandard housing of urban Negroes as due mainly to their own failure to attempt to better themselves. They appear to believe that Negroes simply lack the will to succeed as other minorities have done in preceding generations. In relying on this "free will" explanation, white Americans place the whole burden of Negro disadvantage on Negroes themselves and therewith tend to deny the reality of the problems Negroes face.[4]

Attitudes toward the various legislative proposals presented to our respondents are significantly related to their racial attitudes but the predictability of the former from the latter is not great.[5] There is undoubtedly unreliability and a certain amount of ambiguity in these measures but there is also the fact that the action proposals all involved governmental intervention into racial problems. We know from earlier studies that this introduces an attitudinal dimension which may be quite unrelated to attitudes toward the specific action proposed. Thus many people would be happy to see the salaries of public school teachers raised but they would not want the federal government to subsidize the schools. Similarly, white people who are generally sympathetic and supportive of black demands may not feel that the federal government is the appropriate instrument to meet them.

It is apparent in retrospect that our survey should have devoted more attention to the extremes of white hostility than it did. Our single question regarding counterrioting appears to have added a dimension to our picture of racial attitudes which goes beyond the three measures with which we have been primarily concerned. Reluctance to associate closely with black people, failure to recognize racial discrimination, and disapproval of black demonstrations or disturbances do not necessarily imply hostility. These attitudes are negative and nonsupportive, but the aggressive ill-will which is expressed in a willingness to see active violence against Negroes has quite a different character. Many white people are negative in some degree in their attitudes toward black people, but relatively few are actively hostile. We will undertake in the succeeding chapters to identify the characteristics of these hostile people and to define insofar as possible the circumstances from which their hostility comes.

---

[4]This theme is developed more fully by Howard Schuman in "Free Will and Determinism" *Trans-action*, December 1969, 44-48; *New Society*, June 4, 1970, 959-962.

[5]When the relationship to the action proposals of the three racial attitudes taken together is computed in multiple correlations the coefficients are somewhat elevated, especially among college graduates.

III

THE SOCIAL LOCATION
OF WHITE ATTITUDES

The preceding pages have shown the great diversity which exists among white people in the cities in their attitudes toward racial questions—diversity which defies any attempt to represent these attitudes in a simple descriptive statement.

We now undertake to explore the background of these attitudes, to draw on the information from our survey to provide an answer to the question of why it is that white people in the cities differ so greatly in their orientation toward race. Ideally we should have available a life history of each of our respondents so that we might trace the development of these attitudes from early childhood. This we obviously do not have, but we do have a wide range of information about the geographical origins of each individual, his religious and national attachments, his present occupational and economic circumstances, his educational experience, as well as, of course, his age and sex. This chapter will be concerned with ascertaining the extent to which differences in racial attitudes can be "explained" by reference to these attributes of social location and experience.

Provenience

About half of the white people living in the 15 large cities of the survey were born in the city where they now live. The others came variously from other large cities (18 percent), small cities (10 percent), small towns (14 percent), or farms (5 percent). These points of origin are, of course, scattered throughout the country.

Since the problem of race in this country has historically had a strong regional quality we may begin our search for an explanation of attitudinal differences by comparing people whose early years were spent in different regions. When we look at the attitudes toward interracial contact, the prevalence of discrimination, and the black protest and then the several action programs which our interview proposed, we find a rather consistent picture. In general, people whose early life was spent in the western or New England states are most positive in their responses to these inquiries. Then follow those from the Middle Atlantic States. Those who grew up in the Midwest or the South are the most negative, with Southerners being particularly resistant to change (Table III-1). One must remember that most of these people are still living in the region where they grew up, and of those who are not, many have lived in their present location a very long time. Thus, our data do not give an accurate representation of racial attitudes in the different regions, rather they show the attitudes of people of different regional origins now living in these northern cities.

Despite the attenuation that one might expect in the attitudes of people who move into a different location, it is clear that part of the difference we have seen in the racial attitudes of urban white people comes from the individual's early background. People who grew up in the South and now live in northern cities, for example, still tend to display the attitudes characteristic of that region. People raised in New England and the West, not all living in those regions at the present time, are most positive in their racial orientation. These differences are in some cases substantial, as for example in acceptance of interracial contact, and they are least impressive in the measure which is least specifically racial, attitudes toward federal aid to the cities. In general, we may conclude that regional origin shows a consistent influence on all of these attitudes except that bearing on federal aid.

When our white respondents are divided according to the size of the community in which they grew up, we again find consistent differences in their racial attitudes, although they tend to be rather small. As Table III-2 demonstrates, people from a farm background are generally least positive in their racial orientation, while those from large cities are most positive. Similar differences appear when we compare people from different backgrounds in their attitudes toward proposals for action. In general, large city people are most favorable toward positive action and farm people are least.

TABLE III-1

Racial Attitudes According to Region of Origin[a]

| Racial Attitudes | *"In what state did you live longest during the first ten years of your life?"* | | | | |
	New England	Middle Atlantic	Midwest	South	West
Favor interracial contact Scale positions 1, 2 & 3	77	61	51	30	83
Perceive much discrimination Scale positions 1, 2 & 3	67	60	57	49	65
Sympathetic to black protest Scale positions 1, 2 & 3	53	38	35	29	65
Favor civil rights legislation Scale positions 1 & 2	66	59	42	41	63
Favor federal aid to cities Scale positions 1 & 2	63	66	49	58	70
Prefer improvement of Negro conditions as long-term solution	64	60	52	46	72
Condone counterrioting	1	4	6	7	1

[a]In this table and those following we have attempted to divide the attitude distributions into approximate halves and we show here the proportion of people in each region falling in the positive half. The actual scale positions represented are shown in each case.

TABLE III-2

Racial Attitudes According to Size of
Community of Origin

Racial Attitudes	Large city	Small city	Small town	Farm
Favor interracial contact	62	59	58	55
Perceive much discrimination	60	63	54	42
Sympathetic to black protest	37	39	37	30
Favor civil rights legislation	57	45	45	44
Favor federal aid to cities	63	54	61	44
Prefer improvement of Negro conditions	58	53	53	48
Condone counterrioting	4	4	7	4

A comparison of this table to the preceding one raises the question as to whether the differences associated with region of origin do not in fact result from the presence of more rural people from some regions than from others. Specifically, it might be argued that the position of people of southern origin in Table III-1 reflects the presence of many people of rural background from the South. Since only a fifth of the white Southerners in these northern cities grew up on farms or in small towns, however, this seems not to be the case. We know from other studies that white people living in a rural situation, especially in the South, tend to hold less favorable racial attitudes than one finds among city-bred people. The attitudes of people of farm origin now living in these large cities differ, but not greatly, from those of the other residents. Perhaps the long residence of some of these farm people in the cities has reduced a difference which was originally more impressive. Something remains, however, and it is not simply a reflection of differences between regions.

National Origin and Religion

There is a history of bad blood between American Negroes and the various immigrant groups which came into the northern cities to compete for jobs. The New York riots of 1863, which began as a protest by Irish immigrants against the Civil War draft, turned into a race riot during which hundreds of black people were killed. The race riots of this century have been variously associated with the Poles and other immigrant groups who lived in close proximity to urban Negroes and in only marginally better economic circumstances. It is commonly assumed that these traditional animosities provide the source of much of the racial tension present today.

We have no comprehensive evidence regarding the racial attitudes of national groups in this country at earlier periods of time; for the most part, we must rely on anecdotal and journalistic reports of racial conflict. If there were ever substantial differences in the attitudes of these groups the fact is that the differences we find today are rather small. We have compared the major national groups in Table III-3, having first removed all persons of the Jewish religion for reasons which will become evident, and the only consistent divergence we find is among people of Polish descent.

As we see, urban residents of Polish ancestry are more negative than other national groups on most of these measures and the difference is particularly sharp in their lack of sympathy for the various aspects of the black protest. On the other hand, they are not any more disposed to countenance white violence than the other groups and their attitudes toward programs

TABLE III-3

Relation Between Racial Attitudes and Country of Origin
(Jewish respondents excluded)

Racial Attitudes	*"What country did most of your ancestors come from (besides America)?"*				
	Germany	Great Britain	Ireland	Poland	Italy
Favor interracial contact	60	57	56	45	52
Perceive much discrimination	54	52	59	50	57
Sympathetic to black protest	37	33	39	20	35
Favor civil rights legislation	51	48	53	35	45
Favor federal aid to cities	42	47	59	56	67
Prefer improvement of Negro conditions	52	50	55	43	59
Condone counterrioting	5	6	6	3	5

of federal aid are more favorable than those of the older, more advantaged Germans and British. It would be an exaggeration to conclude that any of these groups is qualitatively different from the others in its racial outlook; the resemblance is more impressive than the contrast. They are not precisely the same, however, and it is apparent that the attitudes of Polish-Americans have a special character.[1]

Slightly over half of the white residents of these northern cities identify themselves as Catholic, something over a quarter are Protestant, one in eight is Jewish, and four percent say they have no religion. As we see in Table III-4, the differences between Catholics and Protestants in their response to racial questions are very minor; the only issue on which they differ visibly is in the greater willingness of Catholics to support federal aid to the cities. As we have remarked earlier, this is only tangentially a racial question and the greater reluctance of Protestants to support such a program may reflect the persistence of individualistic ideas based on earlier Calvinist ideologies of self-sufficiency.

The pattern of Jewish attitudes presents a striking contrast to that

---

[1] A similar finding is reported by Greeley from a 1963 survey of American Catholics. See Greeley, A. M., *Why Can't They Be Like Us*. New York: Institute of Human Relations, 1969, 46.

of Catholics and Protestants; Jews are consistently more positive in their orientation toward these racial issues. It is not surprising to find that our Jewish respondents also are considerably more favorable to the suggested programs of federal aid than the adherents of the other religions are. This is consistent with earlier studies of public attitudes toward welfare legislation and taken with the data from our racial questions it suggests that Jews as a group are characterized by a more integrated structure of social attitudes than we typically find in the general population. The small group of urban white people who say they do not consider themselves to have any religion, two-thirds of them being men, resemble urban Jews in most respects, although they have no special interest in federal aid programs.

TABLE III-4

Racial Attitudes According to Religion

Racial Attitudes	Catholic	Protestant	Jewish	No Religion
Favor interracial contact	54	56	72	68
Perceive much discrimination	56	51	74	75
Sympathetic to black protest	33	36	51	57
Favor civil rights legislation	46	44	67	63
Favor federal aid to cities	58	46	83	56
Prefer improvement of Negro conditions	53	50	68	61
Condone counterrioting	6	5	1	4

The resemblances and differences we have seen between the three major religious groups raise questions as to the way in which religious identification influences racial attitudes, if indeed it does at all. We have seen in earlier studies that group influence depends on two factors; the clarity and force with which the group is projecting a message and the strength of the individual member's identification with the group.[2] We have no information about any statements regarding race which our white respondents may have heard in their churches, but we do have a rough measure of how closely they were attached to their church. Each indi-

---

[2]See, for example, Converse, P. E. and Campbell, A., "Political Standards in Secondary Groups," in *Group Dynamics,* D. Cartwright and A. Zander (Eds.). New York: Harper and Row, 1968.

vidual was asked how often he attended church and their answers ranged from regularly to never. If the churches these people attend are taking a clear and forceful position on questions of race and if this message is influencing attitudes, we should expect to find this influence most apparent among those people who are in closest contact with their church. Thus, if the churches were to translate the doctrine of the brotherhood of man into an endorsement of racial equality and the measures needed to bring it about, we might expect those churchgoers with a close attachment to their church to reflect this influence.

When we actually examine the data from our survey in Table III-5, we find that church attachment shows no consistent relationship to racial attitudes except to that which specifically implies hostility toward Negroes. Protestants and Catholics who never attend their church are clearly more likely than those who do to countenance the prospect of white violence against Negroes. On the other attitudinal measures, those that do not necessarily imply ill will or hostility, these differences do not appear. Thus, in acceptance of interracial contact, the perception of discrimination, support of the black protest and positive response to legal and economic programs of aid, Protestants and Catholics who are closest to their church do not differ from those who are furthest away. Church attendance, with whatever exposure to church doctrine this may imply, apparently has no influence on these attitudes, but it does reduce the acceptability of strong-arm or violent actions by whites in response to the black protest.

The small size of our Jewish sample does not permit a detailed comparison of a similar kind among people of this faith. Grouping the data more broadly, however, we find no indication that frequency of attendance of religious services has any relationship to the racial outlook of Jews. It is apparently not so much the purely religious aspects of being Jewish which are responsible for the pattern of generally positive attitudes which we have seen. As members of a self-conscious subculture, subject to some aspects of the minority situation which Negroes experience, these urban Jews apparently acquire these attitudes as part of a generally "liberal" orientation toward social and political issues. It may be argued that this orientation reflects basic values which are implicit in the Jewish religion but it is clear that close association with the synagogue as adults does not contribute anything unique to this racial outlook.

Occupation and Income

One of the explanations most commonly given for the presence of racial resentment and hostility is that it derives basically from economic

TABLE III-5

Relation of Racial Attitudes to Frequency
of Church Attendance by Protestants and Catholics

Racial Attitudes	Catholic Church Attendance				Protestant Church Attendance			
	Regularly	Often	Seldom	Never	Regularly	Often	Seldom	Never
Favor interracial contact	56	51	49	61	58	47	59	54
Perceive much discrimination	56	62	53	60	54	42	54	42
Sympathetic to black protest	32	45	38	19	40	26	33	31
Favor civil rights legislation	47	43	47	39	47	39	46	45
Favor federal aid to cities	57	66	60	57	36	40	56	49
Prefer improvement of Negro conditions	55	56	45	57	54	40	52	46
Condone counterrioting	5	6	9	13	2	2	5	12

competition. The historical use of the Negro as a strikebreaker and the wartime importation of southern black people into the northern industrial centers with the subsequent problems of unemployment have given this thesis particular meaning in this country. The exclusion policies of many of the craft unions still provide a convincing illustration of the determination of advantaged white workers to protect themselves from black competition.

The history of the black worker in the cities is too well-known to require more than brief review here. Discriminated against, exploited, and often unemployed, for decades he has occupied the bottom rungs of the occupational ladder. Since World War II, however, with the rise of integrated industrial unions, a substantial reduction in the racial differential in educational achievement, an expanding economy, and stronger legal protection against discrimination on the job, this situation has been changing. The average income of a black family has moved from around 40 percent of that of the average white family to around 60 percent and there has been a dramatic shift of black employment from the unskilled occupations into the skilled, clerical, and professional occupations. The differences between white and black are still large, of course, as we will see in Chapter IV, but there has been an unmistakable upgrading in the occupations of Negroes.

One may speculate as to the probable reaction of white workers to this upward movement by Negroes. If direct competition for jobs is the determining factor, we might expect to find resistance and resentment at those job levels into which Negroes are moving. Perhaps those white workers at the lowest occupational levels who have seen black workers move past them are most sensitive to the changes they see. Professional workers at the top of the ladder might feel least threatened at the prospect of competing with black people.

When we actually compare the attitudes of white people at these different occupations we find that none of these plausible expectations is fulfilled (Table III-6). The racial orientation of white people at different occupational levels differs very little, with the single dramatic exception of clerical workers. These lower level white-collar employees are clearly more positive in their attitudes regarding race than any of the other occupational groups. Indeed, the only one of our measures in which they do not differ from the other occupational groups is the one which is not explicitly racial in content, attitude toward federal aid to the cities.

There is no immediately convincing explanation as to why clerical workers should differ so markedly from other white workers, especially from the other white-collar occupations, sales and the professions. As an area currently being seriously invaded for the first time by black workers,

TABLE III-6

Racial Attitudes According to Occupation

Racial Attitudes	Service	Operatives	Crafts, Foremen	Sales	Clerical	Managerial	Professional
Favor interracial contact	50	50	50	55	72	54	56
Perceive much discrimination	55	56	53	50	72	60	51
Sympathetic to black protest	25	22	29	46	41	35	49
Favor civil rights legislation	28	50	45	46	60	44	53
Favor federal aid to cities	61	51	62	53	61	58	60
Prefer improvement of Negro conditions	55	45	51	49	61	54	64
Condone counterrioting	6	10	5	3	4	4	2

one might not have been surprised to find it characterized by generally negative reactions. The contrary is true. It would be plausible to attribute the unique quality of the clerical people to the fact that they are largely high school graduates. But as we shall see later, a high school education has very little effect on these attitudes. We know that most clerical workers are women, but when we compare men and women in this occupational status we do not find any consistent differences in racial attitudes. It may be that there is some special quality of the work situation of clerical employees which fosters the development of positive racial attitudes; our survey does not identify it.

TABLE III-7

Racial Attitudes According to Family Income

Racial Attitudes	Less than $3,000	$3,000 to $5,999	$6,000 to $8,999	$9,000 to $13,999	$14,000 and over
Favor interracial contact	59	59	55	58	60
Perceive much discrimination	53	55	56	60	66
Sympathetic to black protest	32	36	35	41	42
Favor civil rights legislation	52	47	49	51	52
Favor federal aid to cities	59	69	55	57	59
Prefer improvement of Negro conditions	54	52	52	59	52
Condone counterrioting	4	9	5	4	4

Occupation and family income are related, but they are not as closely related as one might expect. The presence of double incomes in many families introduces a complication, and recent trends in wage levels have reversed certain long-standing differentials. Occupational status has become a very imperfect indicator of family income. Whatever income level does tell us about people, it tells us surprisingly little about their racial orientation. The general patterns of racial attitudes are so similar among people of high, medium, and low income that knowing family income helps us very little in explaining differences in racial orientation

Age and Education

We turn finally to the two aspects of individual difference which would appear to hold the greatest promise for our understanding of the nature of racial attitudes. Age is a consideration of particular importance because it permits us to see the generational shift in these attitudes and perhaps to foresee the trend of changes in the future. Formal education, as one of the major acculturating forces in our society, has the power to produce far-reaching changes in social attitudes and its influence in the area of race is of the greatest interest.

Table III-8 compares the attitudes and experiences of white men and women who differ in age. There are some irregularities in the data, resulting in part at least from dividing the total sample into so many small segments, but there is a generally consistent pattern. Looking first at men and at the three basic racial attitudes, we see that there is a moderate downward slope in positive attitudes in the older age cohorts, most apparent in sympathy for the black protest. This slope also appears in attitudes toward the various action proposals. There is also a clear tendency for younger men to report having Negro friends more often than older men. Excluding the very young for the moment, we see no age relationship to approval of white counterviolence among men, and very little relationship to the perception of racial hostility. The 16 to 19 year olds are generally more positive than older men, especially in their sympathy for black protesters, but they differ relatively little from the adjacent age decade (20 to 29) on any of the other measures except those having to do with counterrioting and perceived hostility. Young men under 20 are very much more willing to condone white violence and clearly more likely to see much hostility between the races. Aside from these specific exceptions, we may conclude that younger men tend to be more positive in their racial orientation than older men, but the differences are not remarkable.

The picture of women's attitudes resembles that of men; we see some moderate changes with age. The young women under 20 are generally more positive on the attitudinal measures than older women are, but they do not show the high tolerance of white violence and the strong perception of interracial hostility which we saw among very young men.

Table III-8 reveals a gradual, and for the most part not very dramatic, increase in the positive character of racial attitudes as we move from the older decades to the younger. The age effect is substantial in the extent of sympathy for the black protest and in the amount of friendly contact with black people. Teenage youth of both sexes are generally more positive than older men and women, although the high proportion of very

TABLE III-8

Racial Attitudes According to Age

Racial Attitudes	MEN					
	16-19	20-29	30-39	40-49	50-59	60-69
Favor interracial contact	68	69	69	56	50	65
Perceive much discrimination	79	70	64	44	54	47
Sympathetic to black protest	62	49	39	25	29	24
Favor civil rights legislation	45	48	45	38	35	34
Favor federal aid to cities	68	67	57	54	51	49
Prefer improvement of of Negro conditions	58	57	55	56	44	49
Condone counterrioting	21	6	7	4	7	5
Have friendly contact with Negroes Scale positions 1 & 2	67	60	48	46	45	38
Perceive much dislike between the races Scale positions 4 & 5	28	17	18	16	22	23

	WOMEN					
	16-19	20-29	30-39	40-49	50-59	60-69
Favor interracial contact	63	58	50	51	47	52
Perceive much discrimination	67	71	61	50	46	48
Sympathetic to black protest	59	51	37	32	23	26
Favor civil rights legislation	52	44	43	33	35	39
Favor federal aid to cities	79	69	48	56	55	54
Prefer improvement of Negro conditions	71	68	54	49	46	53
Condone counterrioting	2	3	2	3	5	1
Have friendly contact with Negroes	57	50	44	30	29	27
Perceive much dislike between the races	14	15	12	17	15	17

young men who countenance white violence is a conflicting note. The simple picture of a traditional culture pattern which is gradually fading as the generations succeed each other is consistent with our data, but it is apparent that age alone does not provide a very complete explanation of the profound differences in racial attitudes which we find among individual white people.

We can take an important step toward illuminating this pattern of age differences by examining the possible influence of formal education on racial attitudes. We know that the age decades in Table III-8 differ markedly in their educational achievement and especially in the proportions of their numbers who have experienced some part of a college education. While the proportion of the cohort now 60 to 69 who entered college in this country during the decade following World War I was less than one in ten, the corresponding proportion of the 20-29 cohort is over one in three. In other words, the younger cohorts are better educated as well as being younger, and it behooves us now to look at the effects of age and education independently.

The consequences of this separation of age and education are dramatic. Figure III-1 demonstrates the racial attitudes of men and women, below 40 years of age and above 40, with educational achievement ranging from no more than grade school through a college degree. The 16-19 year old cohort has been omitted since this group is small and has not completed its educational achievement. The configurations of the figures representing the three racial attitudes are basically similar, and they show the following facts.

1.   Among older men the relationship between racial attitudes and years of formal schooling is very weak. Among men over 40, years in school is a very imperfect indicator of attitudes toward race. The pattern is similar among older women except among college graduates, who are clearly more positive than other women of their generation and who are also more positive than college men of their age group.

2.   Within the pre-40 generation the racial attitudes of men and women with college experience are substantially and consistently more positive than men and women of lesser education. The attitudes of educational levels below college do not differ consistently from one level to the next, although

young white people with no more than a grade school education are very insensitive to discrimination and very unsympathetic to the black protest.[3]

3. While the college experience appears to have had a greater impact on racial attitudes in the last 20 years than it had in the preceding generation, the high school experience seems not to have changed over this time period. Young people whose education ended with high school are not very different in their orientation toward race than older people of comparable schooling.

4. The relationship of age to racial attitudes which we found in Table III-8 is contributed almost entirely by people of college education who appear in increasing numbers in the younger decades. If we remove all college people from Table III-8 the relationship of attitudes with age virtually disappears.

These general conclusions are extended by a similar analysis of attitudes toward proposals for action regarding racial issues (Figure III-1). Attitudes toward civil rights legislation follow the same pattern as the three basic attitudes, little difference between educational levels below college for either younger or older generations, but a clear separation among younger college people, especially men. The configuration of preference for improving the conditions of urban Negroes rather than exerting more rigid police control as the long-term answer to the riot problem has the same features, although less sharply. The proportions of the white population who recommend counterviolence are so small it is difficult to establish group differences, but it seems clear that college people of both generations are the least likely to be attracted by this prospect and young people of limited education are the most.

---

[3]It should be noted that the samples of white men and women under 40 with no high school are very small (26 and 30 cases, respectively) and are consequently relatively unreliable. It is also significant that approximately a quarter of these people are of southern origin as compared to less than 10 percent of the total sample.

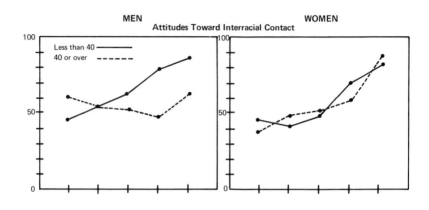

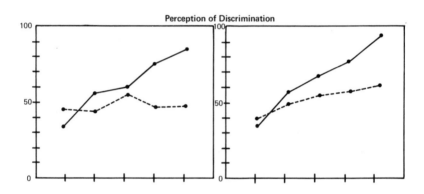

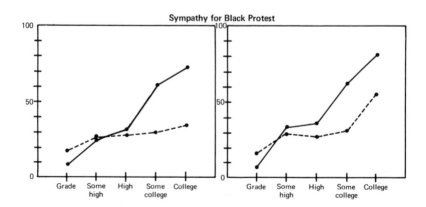

Figure III-1. Racial Attitudes According to Sex, Age and Education

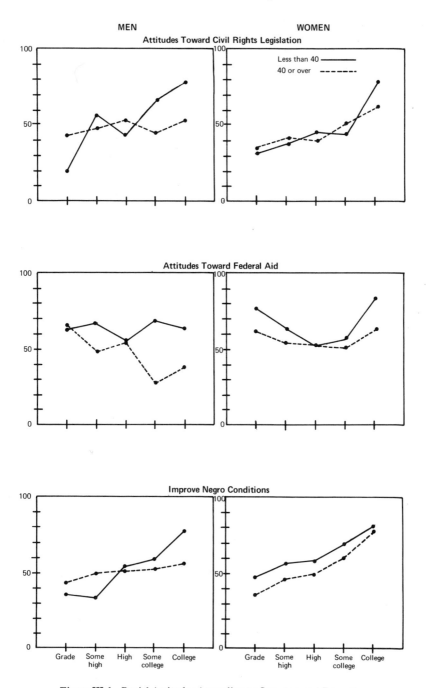

Figure III-1. Racial Attitudes According to Sex, Age and Education

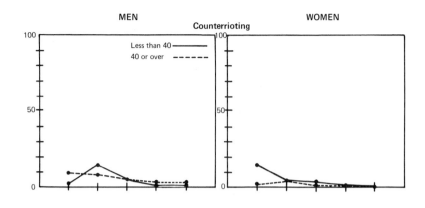

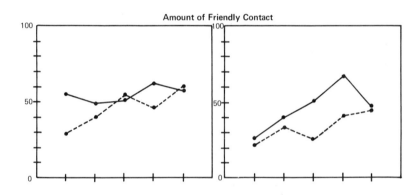

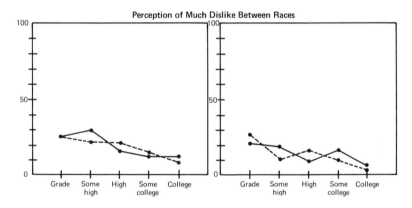

Figure III-1. Racial Attitudes According to Sex, Age and Education

The pattern of attitudes toward federal aid to the cities is obviously quite different. Young people of both sexes are somewhat better disposed to such programs than older people but their approval has no relationship to their educational level. Among older men there is a clear tendency for those with college training to be more disapproving than the rest, but this relationship is not found among older women. We have remarked earlier that attitudes toward federal aid, being essentially economic, seem to derive from a different base than do the racial attitudes and, as we see here, they do not relate in the same way to age and education.

Of the two final measures, amount of friendly contact with black people shows a modest relationship to educational level among older people, but not among younger. Older men and women are moderately more likely to have black friends the more education they have. Young men are about equally likely to have black friends whatever their education may be. While young women are somewhat more likely to report having black friends than older women are, this difference is not found at all educational levels. The perception of widespread dislike between the races is quite clearly related to educational level; people of limited education are much more likely to see "most or nearly all" white and black people disliking each other than are college graduates. These perceptions do not differ by generation, however, young people are no more positive in their evaluation of the extent of racial hostility than older people. Neither do women differ from men in this respect.

From this complex display of data we come to a general conclusion regarding the relative contribution of age and education to the quality of racial attitudes within the white population. Age in itself explains relatively little of the diversity of attitudes which exists among white adults. Much of the evidence of a greater inclination among people under 40 to see racial matters more positively than older people disappears once the effect of education is removed. Indeed, one of the few indications of any specifically youthful attitude is a greater willingness among young men under 20 to countenance white violence against Negroes.

For that part of the white population whose formal schooling has not gone beyond high school (about three-quarters of these urban white people) years in school has only a modest relationship to racial attitudes. These people vary a great deal, of course, in their views on racial questions and we must assume that their individual viewpoints were determined for the most part by their family background, their friends, their personal experiences, and other idiosyncratic influences. The fact that they went to high school or finished high school has surprisingly little effect on the general distribution of their attitudes. There also appears to have been little generational change; those who took a high school diploma after World War II look very much like those who graduated before the War.

It seems apparent that for the past several generations the white high schools of this country have taken a conservative position on the racial issue. For the most part they appear to have accepted the prevailing culture of race relations and racial attitudes in the communities which they serve, and raised no questions about it. The attitudes of young people now in the 16 to 19 year cohort suggest that this picture may be changing. White teenagers in these northern cities, especially girls, are visibly more positive in their racial attitudes than the older white generations. This difference may be due in part to the fact that all these young people are being educated in metropolitan schools, whereas some part of the older cohorts were students in small towns or rural areas in which prevailing racial norms were less positive. It may also be true, although we have no direct evidence to support the assumption, that the last few years have witnessed a change in the metropolitan schools and that our 16 to 19 year olds have in fact been exposed to a different view of race than would have been true in earlier years. It is also possible, of course, that the generally more sympathetic attitudes expressed by these very young people are part of a youthful idealism that will fade quickly once these people are absorbed into the culture of adult life.

How are we to evaluate the apparent shift in racial attitudes we have seen in the postwar generation of college-educated white people? Do these new attitudes represent a true break with tradition and are they the forerunners of a more widespread change in the pattern of racial attitudes in America? The answers to these questions regarding long-term trends can only be known precisely through a longitudinal study; of course, no such study has been done. There are, however, several lines of evidence which give us some basis for judging whether the attitudes we have found among young college people represent a genuine trend. We can look first at the studies done of college students over the past 40 years. Evidence from studies of college populations during the 1930's is not voluminous but it appears to demonstrate that on "liberal" campuses such as Bennington[4] and Oberlin[5] visible shifts toward more positive attitudes toward Negroes occurred between the freshman and senior years. But in colleges without such a "liberal" at-

[4]Newcomb, T. M., *Personality and Social Change.* New York: Holt, 1943.

[5]Murphy, G. and Likert, R., *Public Opinion and the Individual.* New York: Harper, 1938.

[6]Jones, V., "Attitudes of College Students and the Changes in Such Attitudes During Four Years in College," *Journal of Educational Psychology, 29,* 1938, 114-134. 114-134.

mosphere no such change took place.[5,6]   Since World War II, studies of student populations in a variety of institutions have uniformly found positive changes during the undergraduate years.[7]

We can also ask whether the relationships between college education and positive racial attitudes which we see in our current data existed at the time our present over-40 generation was under 40. The earliest survey of public attitudes regarding race from which relationships with education can be drawn appears to have been a study carried out by the National Opinion Research Center in 1944. As reported by Stember, this survey found rather mixed results in comparing the beliefs and attitudes of white people of different educational levels.[8]   While college people were somewhat more positive in some respects than people of lower education they did not differ in others. This was a national survey which cannot be compared directly to our sample of large cities and we do not have available a comparison of older and younger people. However, these 1944 data do not give much indication of strong educational differences and it seems unlikely that we would have found distinctively positive racial attitudes among young college people at that time.

Some evidence of the persistence of the college influence may be obtained if we look more closely at our own data to see to what extent racial attitudes change during the years following the college experience. We can do this by examining the attitudes of college people by their decade of life. The critical decades in this comparison are the twenties and thirties, the first ten years out of college and the second. As we see in Figure III-2, attitudes toward interracial contact and perceptions of discrimination are equally positive among college people in their thirties as they are among those in their twenties; attitudes toward the black protest are somewhat less positive. Thus we do not find a general regression of young attitudes during the first two decades beyond college although we find a sharp drop after that period to a very stable plateau extending from the forties through the sixties.

Finally, we can examine the question of whether the differences we see in the racial attitudes of young college people are due not to their own education but to the educational background in which they were raised. Since we questioned our respondents regarding the formal education of their parents, we are able to classify each respondent as to whether one or both of his parents attended college, one or both graduated from high school but went no further, or neither graduated from high school. The

---

[7]Feldman, K. A. and Newcomb, T. M., *The Impact of College on Students.* San Francisco: Jossey-Bass, 1969.

[8]Stember, C. H., *Education and Attitude Change.* New York: Institute of Human Relations Press, 1961.

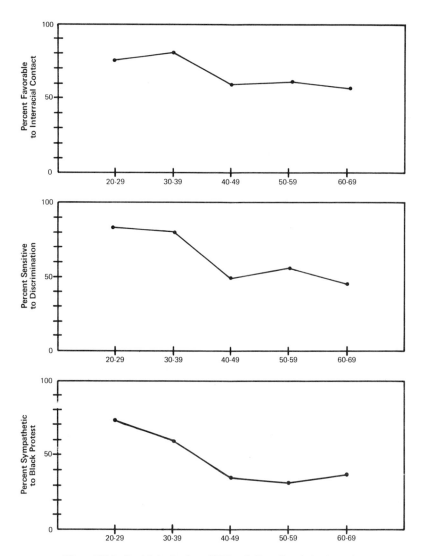

Figure III-2. Racial Attitudes of White College People by Decade of Age

results of this classification, again comparing respondents differing in their own education and age levels, are shown in Figure III-3. This array of data tells us first that among people over 40 years of age, parents' education had no effect on their childrens' racial attitudes. People over 40 whose parents (one or both) attended college are no more or less positive in their answers to our racial questions than people from homes of more modest educational achievement. This supports our earlier supposition that college influence on racial attitudes is a recent development. Among people under 40 the picture is more complex. On all three of our basic attitude scales, young people whose parents did not finish high school are less positive than people of similar age and education who come from more highly educated homes. The attitudes of people under 40 whose parents went to college are not different, however, from those whose parents only finished high school. A college background apparently added nothing to the influences associated with a high school background. The striking fact is, however, that the respondent's own college experience has about the same impact on his racial attitudes whatever the educational level of his family might have been. As we see in Figure III-3, the increment in the proportion offering favorable attitudes is roughly the same for each of the three groups of college people, separated by the educational levels of their parents. The absolute position of those college people from less than high school homes remains lower than that of the two groups with high school graduate and college backgrounds but it, like the others, is clearly more positive than the position of those children of less than high school backgrounds who did not themselves go to college.

It would appear from Figure III-3 that part of the difference in racial attitudes which we find between college and noncollege people in the under-40 generation was probably present before these people actually went to college. Coming disproportionately from homes of higher than average educational level, young people entering college during the last 20 years must have been somewhat more liberated on racial issues than the rest of their cohort at the time they reached the campus. Unpublished data from a recent national survey of high school senior boys permit us to test this hypothesis directly and we do indeed find the expected differential but it is not very substantial.[9] When this sample is divided into those boys who expect to go on to college and those who do not we find the former consistently somewhat more positive than the latter in their answers to ques-

---

[9]This study is being conducted by the Survey Research Center under the direction of Dr. Jerald Bachman. It is designed as a panel study and it is hoped that in due course it will actually be possible to compare the attitudes of those boys who attended college and those who did not.

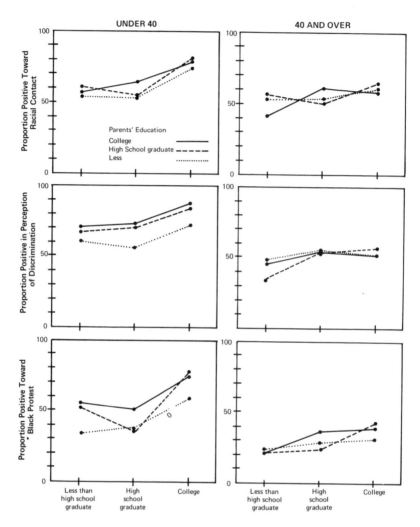

Figure III-3. Racial Attitudes of White People of Different Educational Background According to Their Own Education and Age

tions similar to those asked in the present study. Assuming most of those boys actually do enter college, they will enter differing slightly from their age cohort in their attitudes toward race. It is our belief that when they complete their college careers the difference between their attitudes and those of their cohort will be substantially larger than it was when they entered.

It does not seem likely that the over-40 generation of college students (especially men) ever departed very far from the standard American pattern of racial attitudes of their time. Some small colleges with a liberal orientation apparently succeeded in creating a campus atmosphere which changed student attitudes in this area but these appear to have been exceptional rather than typical. The under-40 college generation does differ from its elders and from young people of lesser education. It is a difference of degree, of course; not all or even most of the postwar college products are positive in their racial attitudes. But they are clearly more positive than the rest of the population and it seems likely they will remain so. If our sense of the trend of movement in American society is correct, they will be succeeded by a generation which is even more positive than they are.

Conclusions

Attitudes and beliefs derive for the most part from the attitudes and beliefs of other people. We assume that the typical white American learns about race from the people around him and that the attitudes he learns are protected and reinforced by the people he chooses to associate with.

We know that the white child in America becomes sensitive to racial differences and develops racial stereotypes and attitudes during his early years.[10] We assume that his family serves as the primary instrument of acculturation, but it is obvious that he is also influenced by the larger community. It is surely impossible to grow up in white America without developing some image of what black people are like and some concept of what their proper relationship to white people should be. The family may be relatively active or passive in indoctrinating its young; it may be in agreement or in conflict with the surrounding society. Whatever attitudes the young person brings from his family setting he will inevitably encounter in due course the racial views of the world around him and he must respond in some way to them.

---

[10] A substantial literature on the development of ethnic attitudes is summarized by Harding, J. *et al., op. cit.*

It is accurate only in a limited sense to speak of American white society as having a common orientation toward race. One may say that the general pattern of attitudes in the United States is different from that in Brazil or even in France, meaning that in general there is greater acceptance of racial equality in those societies than there is in this one. It is evident, however, that within American society (and very probably within the others as well) there are subcommunities which differ substantially in their views on race. Growing up in white America undoubtedly means something racially, but identifying oneself with one or another of the various communities within white America has an independent meaning which must be comprehended in a full understanding of white attitudes.

The doctrine of racial inequality and racial separation which prevailed in white America a hundred years ago has changed at a different pace in different parts of the country and in the different subcommunities within the cities we have studied. In some respects the differences we have noted between the various divisions of society conform to common expectation; it is not surprising, for example, to find that people of southern origin are unusually conservative in their racial views or that Jews are unusually liberal. It is striking, however, how little difference in racial attitudes we find associated with precollege school experience or with attachment to Protestant or Catholic religious institutions. If one thinks of the public schools and the churches as major forces of acculturation in American society one must conclude that their contribution to racial patterns in this country has been to preserve the *status quo*. The role of the churches has been especially remarkable. Despite their historic dedication to the inculcation of moral values, their influence on the racial attitudes of their constituents appears to have been very limited. Churchgoing appears to reduce the acceptability of outright violence against black people but it does not increase willingness to associate with them on an equal basis or create sympathy for their problems.

Racial attitudes are changing most dramatically among those young people who have spent time in the nation's colleges during the past 20 years. The various analyses we have been able to present all tend to support the conclusion that some significant part of the postwar generation of white college students in this country have encountered a different experience on the campus so far as race is concerned than their parents did. We can only speculate as to what brought this change about. Perhaps it was a reflection of the social upheaval of the Depression and the "liberal" philosophy of the New Deal. It may have been influenced by the Second World War with its racial overtones. Certainly it was in part the consequence of the growing importance of the social sciences on campuses throughout the country. Relatively weak before the war, those disciplines which deal specifically with questions of race—social anthropology, social psychology, and sociology—have grown substantially in the past 20 years and their impact on the education of undergraduates has increased accordingly. It is not only that a large proportion of this generation's college students are directly exposed to a critical analysis of their society's culture patterns, including those involving race. The fact is that the whole intellectual life of today's campuses is influenced by the mode of thought and the social criticism associated with the social sciences. The concept of racial justice has become an article of faith for a large proportion of the student body and for some it has become a battleground.

The comparison of communities within the white population which we have presented in this chapter may lead one to wonder which is more impressive, the commonality in the attitudes expressed by these various parts of white society or the differences which appear among them. The overlap in the distribution of attitudes of the groups we have compared is certainly large, but the presence of subcultures within the general pattern is undeniable. Taken as a whole, white America displays a configuration of racial attitudes which differs from that of other societies but within this national pattern social location produces very significant departures from the general norm.

IV

RACIAL DIFFERENCES
IN THE QUALITY OF URBAN LIFE

In the 15 cities with which this study is concerned, there live approximately 4,770,000 black people and 12,280,000 whites. These two populations differ not only in race; they differ in age, place of birth, family structure, and other demographic characteristics; they differ in the conditions of life in which they live, and they differ in their evaluation of the quality of urban life as they know it. Our study was not able to undertake the detailed questioning which would be necessary to achieve the greatest accuracy in reports of family characteristics, housing conditions, income, and other variables. In most cases we were restricted to a single question and our data probably have a relatively large margin of error as a result. The differences between white and black people in the cities are so large in most of these measures, however, that our data seem adequate to make the comparisons in which we are interested.

Demographic Differences

The present racial character of the population of the northern cities is the product of a circulation of white and black people which has been in process for decades. The great migration of black people from the South and of white people to the surrounding suburbs is a familiar story. The consequences of these exchanges of people is seen when we compare the white and black people who now live in the cities.

71

It is apparent at the outset that urban white people are more likely to have been born in the city where they now live, more likely to be long-term residents of the city, and more likely to be above average in age than urban Negroes (Tables IV-1, 2, and 3). Most in-migrant Negroes are from the southern states; the Negro surge into these northern cities during the period of the Second World War is clearly evident. Most in-migrant whites are from the North, typically from the area adjacent to the city where they are now living.

TABLE IV-1

Place of Origin of Residents
of the Fifteen Cities

	WHITE	BLACK
City where now resident	52%	32%
Northeast	9	6
North Central	21	7
South	6	53
West	2	1
Foreign country	10	1
	100%	100%

We need not dwell on the implications of the population profile we see in these tables. Even if black migration to these cities were to taper off and the white flight to the suburbs were to end, there would remain a long-term trend toward a relative increase in the black proportion of the urban population simply because of the youth of the black people now there. Reversals of present trends of movement could alter this trend, if for example, white migration into the cities sufficiently outnumbered black or in case dispersal of black people into the suburbs reached appreciable size, but without rather dramatic changes of this kind it seems very likely that these cities will become increasingly black.

TABLE IV-2

Number of Years in Present City of Residence
in the Fifteen Cities

	WHITE	BLACK
1 year	4%	3%
2- 5 years	8	9
6-10 years	7	9
11-15 years	6	10
16-20 years	6	10
21-30 years	6	16
31-40 years	6	6
More than 40 years	5	5
Whole life	52	32
	100%	100%

The typical white adult in the cities is married and living with his family. This is also true of black people, although the proportion of them who report themselves separated is higher than it is for whites (Table IV-4). In reports of marital status we expect to find general correspondence between the proportions of men and women in the various categories except for the greater number of women than men who report themselves widowed. This expectation is realized in Table IV-4 for our white population, but not for the Negro. The Negro men in our sample are considerably more likely to report themselves as married than are the Negro women and correspondingly less likely to describe themselves as separated or divorced. We do not know whether this discrepancy results from different interpretations placed on these terms by Negro men and women or from a failure of our sampling procedures to locate a proper number of divorced or separated Negro men. The difficulties the Bureau of the Census has in enumerating some sections of the Negro male population suggest that the latter explanation is probably the more important of the two.

TABLE IV-3

Distribution of Age of White and Black Residents
of the Fifteen Cities

	WHITE	BLACK
16-19 years	11%	13%
20-29 years	21	24
30-39 years	15	22
40-49 years	19	19
50-59 years	19	13
60-69 years	15	9
	100%	100%

TABLE IV-4

Marital Status of Black and White Residents
of the Fifteen Cities

	WHITE		BLACK	
	Men	Women	Men	Women
Single	27%	23%	25%	21%
Married	67	64	65	50
Widowed	2	8	3	11
Separated	1	1	5	13
Divorced	3	4	2	5
	100%	100%	100%	100%

The average Negro household in the cities is larger than the average white household, the proportion with six or more members being very considerably higher. As Table IV-5 demonstrates, the urban Negro household is more likely to have children under 16 and less likely to have adults over 40. As we will see later, Negro families in the cities are not only larger than white families, they also occupy less space per family member. The total explanation of crowding in the Negro households of the cities is more complex than we can undertake here, involving as it does the higher birth rate of Negroes, the restriction of Negroes to black areas which are inadequate to accommodate them, and the simple economic inability of the Negro family to rent or buy space comparable to that of the average white person. Whatever the reasons, the typical Negro household in the cities is younger and larger than that of the typical white.

An additional important attribute of the nature of the family structure of Negroes in the cities is revealed when we ask whether the individual lived with both his mother and father until he was 16 years old. We see in Table IV-6 that the majority of black people grew up with both parents, but it is also clear that a third of these urban Negroes have been reared in a broken home and this proportion has not changed appreciably in the last 50 years.[1] Our survey unfortunately did not collect comparable data from the white sample but the extent of racial differences in the composition of urban families is seen in the 1960 census which reports 23 percent of Negro families headed by a woman as compared to 7 percent of the white families.[2]

Finally, we find substantial differences between the white and black populations in their years of formal education. The historical background of these discrepancies is self-evident; the generations of deprivation and denial of equal rights have left their mark. The extent to which that mark has faded becomes apparent, however, when we compare the older and younger generations of the two races (Table IV-7). A racial differential still exists at the college level, but as these and other data show, the difference in the proportions of the young white and Negro cohorts in these cities who will eventually finish high school is not very large.[3]

Conditions of Life

One of the compromises at the Constitutional Convention in 1787 which made it possible for the former colonies to unite into a republic

---

[1]It may be noted that these figures depart substantially from Moynihan's estimate that "it is probable that not much more than one-third of Negro youth reach eighteen having lived all their lives with both parents." See Moynihan, D. P., "Employment, Income and the Negro Family," *Daedalus,* Fall 1965, 761.

[2]U.S. Census: 1960, PC (1) D., U.S., Volume, Table 225, State Volume, Table 140.

[3]The racial discrepancy in median years of school completed is also closing on the national scale. See Taeuber, C., "Population: Trends and Characteristics," in Eleanor B. Sheldon and W. E. Moore (Eds.), *Indicators of Social Change.* New York: Russell Sage Foundation, 1968, 38.

TABLE IV-5

Composition of White and Black Households
in the Fifteen Cities

Number of persons in the household	Under 16		16-25		26-40		Over 40		Total	
	White	Black	White	Black	White	Black	White	Black	White	Black
0	54%	42%	53%	51%	62%	48%	32%	42%	0%	0%
1	18	17	26	24	19	27	18	24	8	8
2	14	14	17	17	18	22	44	27	27	23
3	7	10	2	5	—	1	5	4	20	17
4	4	7	1	2	0	0	—	1	19	16
5	2	4	1	—	0	0	—	—	11	10
6+	1	5	0	—	0	0	0	—	14	25
NA	—	1	—	1	1	2	1	2	1	1
	100%	100%	100%	100%	100%	100%	100%	100%	100%	100%

TABLE IV-6

"Did you always live with both your mother and father until you were 16 years old?"
(IF NO) *"What happened?"*

| | BLACK RESIDENTS | | | |
	16-19	20-39	40 or over	TOTAL
Yes, family intact	65%	63%	64%	64%
No, orphan; unclear	8	4	5	5
No, father absent	21	24	19	21
No, mother absent	5	7	10	8
Not ascertained	1	2	2	2
	100%	100%	100%	100%

was the agreement that black slaves in the southern states should count as three-fifths of a man in determining a state's representation in Congress.   Now nearly 200 years later the descendants of those slaves are paid on the average three-fifths of the income of the average white man.[4]

This does not mean, of course, that all Negroes are living in poverty, that they all do menial work, or that they all live in substandard housing. The economic differentials among black people and the class differences associated with them are well documented. The important fact for us at the moment is that urban Negroes as a group differ substantially from urban whites in the basic economic conditions of their lives: we will consider later the psychological importance of this to the individual Negro and white person.

When we compare the annual income of white and black families in the cities, we find the distribution shown in Table IV-8.   There was undoubtedly a certain amount of error in the reporting of income, but it would not be sufficient to change the general pattern we see.   The average income of these urban Negroes is higher than the national Negro average, but it is plainly less than that of the urban whites.

---

[4]The Economic Report of the President of January 1969 estimates the median income of nonwhite families to be 62 percent of that of white.

TABLE IV-7

Educational Levels of White and Black Residents
in the Fifteen Cities

	WHITE				BLACK			
	16-19	20-39	40-69	TOTAL	16-19	20-39	40-69	TOTAL
Some grade school	1%	2%	9%	6%	1%	5%	27%	13%
Completed grade school	5	3	16	11	3	5	13	8
Some high school	60	19	23	25	68	33	27	35
Completed high school	25	40	30	33	23	38	20	29
Some college	9	20	12	14	5	13	9	11
Completed college	—	16	10	11	—	6	4	4
	100%	100%	100%	100%	100%	100%	100%	100%

TABLE IV-8

Annual Income of White and Black Families in the Fifteen Cities

	WHITE	BLACK
Under $3,000	6%	12%
$ 3,000-$5,999	16	29
$ 6,000-$8,999	27	28
$ 9,000-$13,999	29	18
$14,000 and over	14	7
Not ascertained	8	6
	100%	100%

Table IV-9 compares the employment status of the two races and documents two familiar facts, the greater incidence of unemployment among Negroes and the greater proportion of white women who are not in the labor market.

TABLE IV-9

Employment Status of Whites and Blacks in the Fifteen Cities

	WHITE			BLACK		
	Men	Women	TOTAL	Men	Women	TOTAL
Employed	77%	40%	59%	79%	46%	63%
Retired	8	4	6	6	4	5
Unemployed	2	2	2	5	8	6
Student	13	9	11	10	10	10
Housewife	–	45	22	–	32	16
	100%	100%	100%	100%	100%	100%

Although there have been substantial shifts in Negro employment during the past 20 years toward the white-collar and better-paid occupations, the remaining discrepancy between the races is impressive (Table IV-10). Two out of three of the employed Negroes are in blue-collar or service jobs, while less than half of the white workers are so employed. It is apparent, however, that the discrepancy in the skilled worker, clerical, and professional categories is narrowing.[5]

TABLE IV-10

Occupational Status of Whites and Blacks in the Fifteen Cities

	WHITE			BLACK		
	Men	Women	TOTAL	Men	Women	TOTAL
Unemployed	2%	2%	2%	5%	8%	6%
Laborers	3	–	1	10	*	6
Service workers including private households	5	5	5	12	16	14
Operatives and kindred	16	6	11	27	12	19
Craftsmen, foremen	20	2	11	12	1	7
Sales	5	4	4	1	1	1
Clerical and kindred	9	19	14	10	12	11
Managers, officials and proprietors	12	3	8	4	1	3
Professional, technical	14	5	10	8	6	7
Student, housewife, etc.	14	54	34	11	43	26
	100%	100%	100%	100%	100%	100%

*Less than one percent

---

[5] A detailed statement of these changes in employment patterns may be found in Hodges, Claire C., "The Negro Job Situation: Has It Improved?," *Monthly Labor Review,* January 1969.

Most urban Negro families, two out of three, rent the space they live in; slightly less than half of urban white families rent the space they occupy. One black family in eight lives in a detached single-family house; the corresponding proportion of white families is about one in four. The average number of rooms occupied by black families is not notably smaller than that of white families, but because of the differences in size of families, the ratio of persons to rooms is higher for black families than white (Table IV-11).

TABLE IV-11

Number of Persons per Room
in White and Black Dwellings

	WHITE	BLACK
Fewer people than rooms	65%	51%
About one to one	23	25
One and a quarter persons per room	5	7
One and three-quarters persons per room	5	10
More than one and three-quarters persons per room	1	3
Not ascertained	1	4
	100%	100%

We are unable to provide any assessment of the quality of the housing these urban people occupy. We know that Negro families who rent pay less on the average than white families, but since we cannot be sure that rents in Negro neighborhoods have the same relationship to the quality of the space rented that they have in white neighborhoods, it is not possible to make a direct comparison of white and black housing on the basis of rent alone.

None of this tells us anything new about the lives of white and black people in America. There has never been a time when the income, occupational status, or housing of the black population has equaled the whites. Studies of long-term trends indicate that these differentials are narrowing, but the remaining discrepancies are substantial.

Evaluations of Urban Life

The National Advisory Commission on Civil Disorders observes in the opening paragraphs of its report that "our nation is moving toward two societies, one black, one white." The preceding pages have shown us some of the ways in which the circumstances of life of these two societies differ. They do not live in totally different worlds; there is a great range of characteristics in both races and many whites live very much the same kind of life as many blacks. But taken collectively, the differences are unmistakable.

We now ask what the impact of these differences is on the quality of life as these people experience it. We can give only a limited answer to this question. Our inquiry does not tell us anything, for example, about the more private aspects of life experience such as those associated with marriage or the family and it does not probe with any depth into the intensity of feeling these urban people have about the lives they lead.[6] We did ask a series of questions about the experiences people encounter in the public life of their communities and we can compare the degree of satisfaction expressed by white and black people with them.

We are well aware that satisfaction is a difficult concept and that we might very reasonably have devoted a far greater investment of our interview time to developing measures of satisfaction than we did. We proceed on the assumption that when two people tell us they are satisfied with their public schools, their police force, or their housing they are equivalent in the sense that their present aspiration is close enough to their present achievement that the discrepancy does not create a sense of deprivation and discontent. Their absolute levels of aspiration and achievement may differ greatly but in the sense that two bottles of unequal size may be said to be equally full when both are filled to the top we will treat all those who tell us they are satisfied as being equally satisfied.

Public Services. Every large city undertakes to provide certain services to its citizens, and theoretically it provides these services evenhandedly and without regard to questions of race. But we find that Negroes

---

[6]An inquiry in depth into the quality of urban living would undoubtedly pose serious methodological problems, especially with Negro respondents. From his experience with studies of ghetto youth, Kenneth Clark believes that "the use of standardized questionnaires and interview procedures would result in stylized and superficial verbal responses or evasions. The outstanding finding at this time was that data obtained by these traditional methods did not plumb the depth or the complexities of the attitudes and anxieties, the many forms of irony and rage which form the truth of the lives of the people of Harlem." See Clark, K. B., *Dark Ghetto.* New York: Harper, 1965, xix.

do not find these services as satisfactory as do whites. There is a good deal of complaint in both races about the adequacy of various public services but in every case Negroes are more likely to be critical than whites. As we see in Table IV-12, these criticisms are not indiscriminate complaints about everything the city attempts to do. Garbage collection, for example, is regarded as satisfactory by a substantial majority of both races, but neither race is satisfied with the adequacy of recreation centers for teenagers. Contrary to the observation of the National Advisory Commission on Civil Disorders, which speaks of "the hostility of Negro parents and students toward the school system," the public schools are the source of relatively little serious dissatisfaction and the amount of complaint is not much greater among Negroes than whites. The most controversial service of those concerning which we have information is that of police protection. White people are generally satisfied with the city police;

TABLE IV-12

"I'd like to ask how satisfied you are with some of the main services the city is supposed to provide for your neighborhood. What about the quality of the public schools in this neighborhood—are you generally satisfied, somewhat dissatisfied, or very dissatisfied?"

	Quality of public schools		Parks and playgrounds for children		Sports and recreation centers for teenagers	
	WHITE	BLACK	WHITE	BLACK	WHITE	BLACK
Generally satisfied	48%	42%	50%	30%	34%	24%
Somewhat dissatisfied	15	22	20	26	21	20
Very dissatisfied	9	15	18	27	21	30
Don't know	28	21	12	17	24	26
	100%	100%	100%	100%	100%	100%

	Police Protection		Garbage collection	
	WHITE	BLACK	WHITE	BLACK
Generally satisfied	67%	46%	81%	68%
Somewhat dissatisfied	18	20	8	13
Very dissatisfied	11	26	8	16
Don't know	4	8	3	3
	100%	100%	100%	100%

Negroes are as likely to express dissatisfaction as satisfaction, and a quarter of them say they are "very dissatisfied." As we will see later, the whole area of relations with the police is an aggravated one with the Negro community.

A summary question closed this series of inquiries regarding specific city services and asked for a comparative evaluation of the services received by the respondent's own neighborhood in relation to other parts of the city (Table IV-13). Apparently the majority of these city people are not very sensitive to such differences as may exist in the quality of the services the city provides its various neighborhoods. Of those white people who see any differences, however, two out of three feel they are treated better than average. Among black people, the picture is reversed; two out of three who see differences feel they are worse off than average. These findings are altogether consistent with the results obtained from the preceding questions.

TABLE IV-13

"Thinking about city services like schools, parks and garbage collection, do you think your neighborhood gets better, about the same, or worse service than most other parts of the city?"		
	WHITE	BLACK
Better	18%	10%
About the same	65	61
Worse	8	21
Don't know	9	8
	100%	100%

In order to locate these attitudes regarding city services within the total population, we have compared people of different age, education and income. We do not find a consistent pattern of relationships running through these various questions; age in particular tells us little about differences in these attitudes. There are, however, specific intriguing findings. We see, for example, that satisfaction with the public schools does not vary among white people of different age or education, nor does it vary among black people except among those below 40 who have attended college.

Young black college graduates are very dissatisfied with the quality of the schools their cities provide, much more so than white college people of similar age. Income level, on the other hand, has little relationship to any of these measures except satisfaction with police protection. Low income people of both races, but especially Negroes, are less satisfied with police protection in their neighborhoods than are people of high income level.

A second interesting finding also concerns people of college training. We discover, not surprisingly considering the quality of the neighborhoods in which they live, that white college graduates of both younger and older generations are visibly more likely to feel their neighborhood receives better than average service than do people of less education. Among Negroes, the same result is found among young college people (under 40) but it is not present among older people. Although these young people are very critical of the public schools, they are still far more likely to feel their neighborhood is in general relatively well served by the city than other Negroes are. We will have occasion to remark on other characteristics of this important segment of the Negro population at later points in this presentation. High income people of both races are somewhat more ready to say their neighborhood gets superior service than are those with lower incomes.

Governmental Effort. At the time this study was being carried out there was a great deal of talk in the air about "solving the urban problem." The violent Summer of 1967 was in the very recent past and predictions of worse things to come were commonplace. All levels of government, city, state, and federal, were involved with legislation of one kind or another intended to reduce the likelihood of further violence and, as we have seen, the populations of the cities generally felt some such governmental intervention should occur.

As one might have expected, Negroes found all these efforts less convincing than did white people (Table IV-14). Both races gave their city mayor higher marks for "trying as hard as he could to solve the problems of the city" than they gave the federal government or their state government. But white people were considerably more satisfied with their mayor than black people. Both races gave the federal government credit for greater effort than the state government, white people again complaining less than black people.

The fact that Negroes are less satisfied with the efforts of governmental agencies than white people does not mean that they are hostile to those governmental programs which have been initiated. On the contrary, in evaluating the federal antipoverty programs they are considerably more positive than whites. About one Negro in four reports that some member of his family has participated in one of these programs as compared to one white person in ten, and as Table IV-14 demonstrates, most Negroes believe these programs are doing a good or fair job. White people have had much less direct contact with these programs and almost three times as many of them believe the programs have done a "poor job."

TABLE IV-14

"Do you think the mayor of (CITY) is trying as hard as he can to solve the main problems of the city or that he is not doing all he can to solve these problems? (IF NOT DOING ALL HE CAN) Do you think he is trying fairly hard to solve these problems or not hard at all?"

	WHITE	BLACK
Trying as hard as he can	65%	46%
Fairly hard	16	19
Not hard at all	13	24
Don't know	6	11
	100%	100%

"How about the state government?"

	WHITE	BLACK
Trying as hard as it can	41%	32%
Fairly hard	23	22
Not hard at all	25	32
Don't know	11	14
	100%	100%

"How about the federal government in Washington?"

	WHITE	BLACK
Trying as hard as it can	51%	39%
Fairly hard	21	25
Not hard at all	21	25
Don't know	7	11
	100%	100%

It appears that the differences between whites and Negroes shown in these tables derive from a greater sense of need and higher aspiration for change among blacks than whites. Negroes are more likely to approve the programs which have been started and to feel they should be extended. White people are not as favorable to the start which has been made and not as likely to feel that the various governmental agencies should do more.

TABLE IV-15

"In general, do you think the antipoverty program is doing a good job, a fair job, or a poor job?"	WHITE	BLACK
A good job	17%	38%
A fair job	38	37
A poor job	24	9
Don't know	11	7
Haven't heard of antipoverty program	10	9
	100%	100%

In these evaluations of governmental programs we find very little difference between generations among either the white or black population. When we divide the generations by educational level, however, differences begin to appear. In both races people of higher educational level are more favorably impressed with their mayor's efforts than less educated people. Conversely, college-educated young people of both races are highly critical of their state government; older people show no consistent pattern. There is no clear relationship of education to attitudes toward the federal government's efforts. Among white people the antipoverty program draws most of its criticism from college people, who of course have the least direct contact with it. The same pattern is found among young college Negroes; the attitudes of older Negroes do not vary by education. Family income, which in this urban population is not highly associated with years of formal education, does not relate in any significant way with these attitudes toward the performance of the various governmental agencies.

It is not surprising to find these instances in which people of higher education are most critical of the programs of their legislative agencies.

It is intriguing, however, to discover that when we consider the mayor rather than the state or federal government, it is the poorly educated who are most dissatisfied. This suggests that there is some factor of proximity which brings local politics within the critical range of people of modest education, but excludes more distant abstractions of government in Washington or in the state capitol.

The Police. The violence in the cities during the past few years has brought to focus the confrontation between the people and the police, who in all these cities are largely white. The police are continually being accused by black leaders of having racist attitudes and being abusive toward black people. Many policemen feel that Negroes think of them as enemies although they themselves believe strongly that Negroes are treated at least as well by police and other public officials as other people of similar circumstances.[7]

It is difficult to know from the various episodes which achieve widespread publicity what the actual state of relationship between the police and the black population is. Allegations of police brutality involving black people are not uncommon, but they are very difficult to establish in court and it would be impossible in any case to generalize from an occasional dramatic incident to the whole panoply of police-community relations. We have not undertaken a systematic observation of how the police conduct themselves in the 15 cities of our study, but we have inquired into the way white and black people in these cities perceive the behavior of the police and what they report to be their own experience with them.[8] As we will see, relations with the police is an aspect of urban life which looks quite different to white and Negro citizens.

Our specific questions were framed in terms of complaints about the police and in this sense may be said to have invited criticism of them. We do not take the data to represent precisely the actual number of people who have had unfavorable experiences with the police, but rather as an indication of the image these people have of the police, and we are particularly interested in how these images differ between the white and black populations. We presented a series of hypothetical incidents increasing in seriousness beginning with a question dealing with what we thought would be the most common complaint that might be offered concerning the police—they do not come quickly when called. This was

---

[7]See Rossi, Peter *et al.,* "Between White and Black" in *Supplemental Studies for the National Advisory Commission on Civil Disorders.* Washington: Government Printing Office, 1968.

[8]A comparison of the experiences with the police of the white and black people living in the 15 separate cities is presented by Schuman, Howard and Gruenberg, Barry in "The Impact of City on Racial Attitudes," *American Journal of Sociology, 76,* 1970, 213-261.

followed by questions regarding the show of disrespect and use of insulting language, frisk or search without good reason, and rough treatment in arrest or afterwards. In each case we asked whether the individual thought this sort of thing happened in his neighborhood, whether it had happened to anyone he knew, and whether it had ever happened to him personally. The responses to these questions are summarized in Figure IV-1.

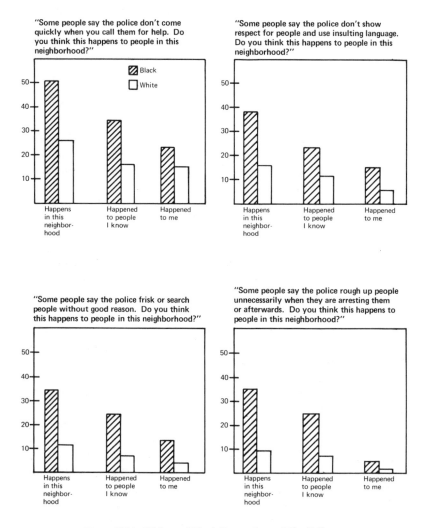

Figure IV-1. White and Black Perceptions of the Police

The most general conclusion which stands out in Figure IV-1 is the fact that Negroes are much more critical of the police than are white people. That is not to say that most Negroes are critical of the police; while proportions ranging up to 51 percent believe these offenses happen in their neighborhoods, much smaller numbers report knowing people to whom these things have happened and even smaller proportions maintain that they have themselves been subjected to such treatment. No one can take any satisfaction from the fact that *only* 13 percent of urban Negroes report having been searched unnecessarily or that *only* 4 percent report having been roughed up by the police. One percent would seem too many. The fact is, however, that the overwhelming majority of urban Negroes have not had this kind of experience. They are much more likely, of course, to believe that the police commit these offenses against other Negroes; reports of such incidents are featured in the Negro press and no doubt circulate widely in the Negro community. The consequence is that unfavorable perceptions of the police are much more prevalent among urban Negroes than unfavorable experiences with them. This is particularly true of the more serious accusation of rough treatment; the number of Negroes to whom this has happened is relatively small, but the number who believe it happens is relatively large.

While white people are much less likely than black people to criticize the police, there is a certain correspondence in the pattern of their complaints. The proportion of white people who believe the police are slow in answering calls is a little over half the proportion of black people who make this complaint and this ratio is not very different for the belief that people they know have had this experience or for the report that they had had the experience themselves. The resemblance declines, however, as we move from complaints about slowness in answering calls, through use of insulting language to unnecessary search and finally rough treatment. It is in the latter cases, involving physical mistreatment by the police, that the discrepancy is greatest between the two races, in both perceptions and reported experiences. It would appear from these data that the police in these cities are several times more likely to put their hands on a black person than on a white.

Although differences in age have not proved very important in the earlier analyses in this chapter, there is no doubt that in contacts with the police age is a very significant factor. As Figure IV-2 makes clear, criticisms of the police are far more common among young people than old and the pattern is very similar among both whites and blacks. Abrasive relations with the police are not only a racial problem in these northern cities, they are also a problem of youth. Young people of both races are not only much more likely to believe the police in their neighborhoods behave badly, they also much more frequently report that they have personally had unpleasant experiences with them. The high incidence of young people in the police records of the large cities suggests that these reports are not unrealistic.

Among white people we do not learn anything additional about the nature of these attitudes and experiences by dividing the under-40 and over-40 generations into educational levels. There are no consistent trends with education within the white population. Among Negroes there is no very substantial educational difference in reactions to slow service or insulting language. College-graduate Negroes are somewhat less likely to criticize the police for unnecessary search or roughness and they are less likely to have personally experienced such treatment. But among Negroes

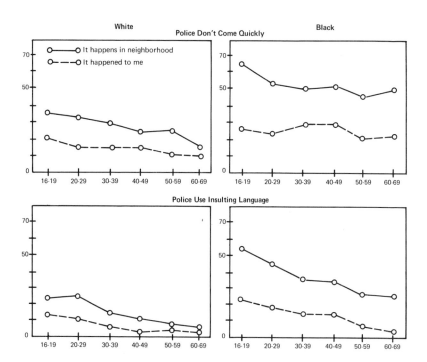

Figure IV-2. Age Differences in White and Black Reports of Experience with the Police

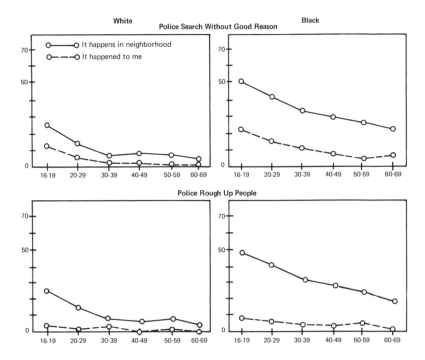

Figure IV-2. Age Differences in White and Black Reports of Experience with the Police

as well as whites, education is far less valuable in explaining attitudes toward the police than is simple chronological age.

We find a generally similar picture when we divide our samples by income status within age levels. White people of varying income, both under and over 40, are about equally likely to complain of police misbehavior in their neighborhood or of police offenses involving themselves or their acquaintances. Black people show a similar pattern. Of particular interest is the distribution of reported incidents of rough treatment by the police. The number of white people who report having been personally abused by a policeman is too small to divide into age and income groups; when asked if they know of such experiences among their friends young white people are more likely to report such episodes than white people 40 or over but the frequency of these reports does not decrease with higher income. The same general pattern is found among black people although incidents of police abuse are reported most frequently by young black men whose family income is less than $3,000.

In view of the commonplace assumption that the police adjust their behavior to the class position of the people with whom they deal these findings seem rather remarkable. Intuitively one would have to expect that a policeman would feel freer to abuse a lower-class person than he would a person of middle-class status. The lack of differences in the reports of lower and higher status Negroes might be explained as a reflection of racial prejudice on the part of white policemen who are equally hostile to black people of all social levels. But it is impossible to apply this reasoning to the white data which also show little difference in complaints of police abuse among people of different educational and income level. Our evidence stands as a contradiction of commonsense expectation and awaits confirmation from other sources.

In this connection we must take note of the fact that these reports of experiences with the police appear to conflict with evidence recently presented by Reiss from observational studies of police behavior. In three of the same cities used in our study Reiss and his assistants actually accompanied the police on their patrols in "high crime precincts" and observed the manner in which the police officers handled the individuals with whom they came in contact. The proportion of these encounters in which the police used an excessive amount of force is very low, but "the rate of excessive force for all white citizens in encounters with the police is twice that for Negro citizens." The 44 individuals observed to be subjected to excessive force were all of lower-class status, and Reiss concludes that "the most likely victim of excessive force is a lower-class man of either race."[9]

It is difficult to make a direct comparison between these two studies, partly because the Reiss study does not have a representative sample of citizens in the cities where its observations were made, but there are at least two obvious discrepancies. We do not find white people more likely to report rough treatment by the police and we do not find such reports exclusively or even predominantly among lower-class people of either race. Direct observation of police roughness is certainly more convincing evidence than subsequent report by the presumed victim, but the concentration of the Reiss observations in the high crime areas of the three cities observed raises problems of comparison which are difficult to resolve.

Stores and Merchants. One further aspect of everyday life in the cities concerns us, shopping in neighborhood stores. The pattern of burn-

---

[9]Reiss, A. J., Jr., "Police Brutality—Answers to Key Questions," *Transaction,* July 1968, 10-19.

ing which occurred in some of the major riots would indicate that some of these local establishments had become the focus of intense resentment. Complaints about overcharging are common in the Negro press and they are apparently not without basis. According to the National Advisory Commission on Civil Disorders, "There are significant reasons to believe that poor households generally pay higher prices for the food they buy and receive lower quality food." Not all Negro households are poor by any means, but the reports of Negroes regarding their experiences in the stores in their neighborhoods are much less favorable than those of whites (Table IV-16).

Urban Negroes are three times as likely to say they are "often" overcharged in the stores in their neighborhoods as are whites. Most white people say they are rarely or never so treated. Negroes are also much more likely to report having been sold goods of poor quality in these stores. It is noteworthy that these urban Negroes are not indiscriminately negative in describing their experiences in these stores; very few of them, for example, say they are often subject to disrespectful treatment in these establishments. In this respect they are much closer to white people than they are in their other complaints.

These complaints about local stores and merchants are slightly more common among people below 40 than among those above 40. The difference is not large, but it appears in both races and at all educational levels. Education itself seems to have little to do with this particular form of dissatisfaction; people with few years of schooling are no more or less likely to criticize their local stores than people with college degrees. People of high income of both races find less to criticize about the price and quality of the goods they purchase in their local stores than lower income people do.

Satisfactions and Dissatisfactions with
Financial Situation, Housing and Job

The objective conditions of life of urban Negroes are clearly different from those of urban whites and they are clearly less advantageous. We now ask what the psychological impact of these circumstances is on these disadvantaged people.

Much of the rhetoric which is heard regarding the attitudes and grievances of the urban Negro seems to be based on the simple assumption that a part of the population whose level of achievement does not come up to some socially recognized standard will inevitably respond to this

TABLE IV-16

"Here are some complaints you hear sometimes about stores and merchants. Will you tell me if these things ever happen to you when you shop in stores in or near this neighborhood? Do you think you are unfairly overcharged for goods, often, sometimes, rarely, or never?"

	WHITE	BLACK
Often	8%	24%
Sometimes	25	32
Rarely	23	14
Never	42	23
Don't shop in neighborhood stores	2	7
	100%	100%

"Do you think you are sold spoiled or inferior goods often, sometimes, rarely, or never?"

	WHITE	BLACK
Often	2%	13%
Sometimes	15	29
Rarely	28	17
Never	53	34
Don't shop in neighborhood stores	2	7
	100%	100%

"In such stores are you treated disrespectfully often, sometimes, rarely, or never?"

	WHITE	BLACK
Often	2%	3%
Sometimes	6	13
Rarely	14	12
Never	76	65
Don't shop in neighborhood stores	2	7
	100%	100%

discrepancy with dissatisfaction and discontent. Since Negroes as a group are less well paid, less well housed, and less well classified occupationally than white people, we should, therefore, expect to find them less well satisfied with these aspects of their lives. Individually we should also expect those whose level of living falls furthest below the general societal standard to feel the greatest sense of deprivation and the keenest feeling of dissatisfaction. We may now examine the extent to which this theory explains the facts.

If we simply compare the distribution of expressions of satisfaction or dissatisfaction among white and black people regarding these basic aspects of their lives, we find the gross differences shown in Table IV-17. It is difficult to say how much difference one might have expected to find in this table, considering the magnitude of the differences in actual conditions of life which underlie them. In relation to the substantial differences in the incomes of white and black people the difference in their degree of satisfaction with income seems remarkably small. Similarly, the lack of difference in the satisfaction of white and black people with their jobs is impressive in light of the frequently-heard complaint that black people are characteristically underclassified in relation to their educational and skill levels. It is housing which is the point of greatest difference in satisfaction levels of whites and Negroes. Negroes are clearly less likely to express themselves as "very satisfied" with their housing than are white people.

If we look within each race to find the extent to which individual satisfaction is associated with actual level of achievement we find a complicated picture. We may use as a measure of achievement either of three indicators, income, education, or occupation and we discover that the pattern of relationships between satisfaction and achievement differs somewhat from one of these indicators to another.

In Figure IV-3 we have divided our white and black samples by annual income and compared the levels of satisfaction reported by people under 40 and over 40 in the successive income brackets. Looking first at the curves of satisfaction with income we see that they conform quite well to the simple proposition that as achievement rises satisfaction rises. The pattern is very similar for both whites and blacks as are the absolute values of satisfaction within comparable income brackets. Among people over 40 race seems to have nothing to do with satisfaction with income; Negroes and whites of this age who have the same income are equally satisfied with it. Among younger people Negroes are a little less likely to call themselves "pretty well satisfied" than are whites who have the same income.

TABLE IV-17

Satisfactions with Conditions of Life
of Urban Whites and Blacks

"In general, would you say you are pretty well satisfied with your family's present financial situation, more-or-less satisfied, or not satisfied at all?"

	WHITE	BLACK
Pretty well satisfied	52%	44%
More-or-less satisfied	34	30
Not satisfied at all	14	26
	100%	100%

"Considering the education and skill you have (had) do you think your job is (was) about right or do you think you belong (belonged) in a job with higher pay and responsibility?"

	WHITE	BLACK
About right	47%	45%
Higher pay and responsibility	15	20
Don't know	3	3
Never in work force	35	32
	100%	100%

"Would you say you are very satisfied, fairly satisfied, somewhat dissatisfied, or very dissatisfied with the housing you (and your family) now have?"

	WHITE	BLACK
Very satisfied	52%	34%
Fairly satisfied	31	34
Somewhat dissatisfied	10	18
Very dissatisfied	6	13
Don't know	1	1
	100%	100%

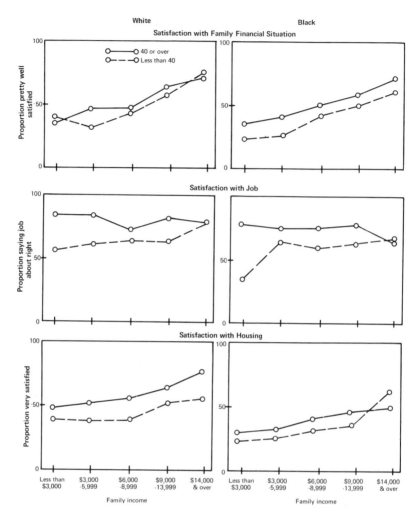

Figure IV-3. Relation of Satisfactions with Housing, Job and Family Financial Situation to Level of Income

We find a quite different pattern when we look at satisfaction with employment. In this case the curves for both white and Negro are basically flat, with the exception of a very low level of job satisfaction among young Negroes of very low income. Job satisfaction does not increase with income and with the exception noted the satisfaction levels of whites and

Negroes in the same income bracket are very similar. Job satisfaction as we have measured it seems to depend neither on race nor on income.[10]

Satisfaction with housing presents still a different picture. There is a moderate relationship between income and satisfaction with housing in both races, not as sharp as between income and satisfaction with income but quite consistent. However, with one exception, Negroes of all income levels are clearly less satisfied with their housing than white people of equal income. The exception is young high-income Negroes who are much more satisfied with their housing than Negroes of lower income and equal in their satisfaction level to young white people of similar income. Race obviously does have something to do with satisfaction with housing; when we take away the effect of income and age we still find a pronounced racial difference.

We may note that in all of the six charts of Figure IV-3 people over 40 tend to be more satisfied with their life circumstances than people under 40. The difference is not great but it is very consistent and equally characteristic of both races. One might be tempted to conclude that older people are more satisfied because they have more to be satisfied with but this can hardly be defended in view of the fact that the difference in satisfaction level is about as great between those who have little, in terms of income, as those who have much. It may be alternatively that people over 40 have learned to accept what they have and no longer aspire so intently for more. Younger people, still in the most mobile period of their careers, may be pursuing aspirations which are further removed from their present achievements and may not yet have adjusted these aspirations downward as considerations of reality may eventually require that they do.

In Figure IV-4 we have taken educational level as a measure of achievement and compared the satisfaction levels with income, job and housing of the different educational strata in each race. We find no evidence in Figure IV-4 of any tendency for these measures of satisfaction to be positively associated with educational achievement. There is a suggestion of a decrease in job satisfaction in the higher educational brackets but this is offset by a reversal of this curve among Negro college graduates. We find again, however, that satisfaction with income and

---

[10]A recent review of the literature regarding job satisfaction makes clear that different measures of this variable produce quite different results. It should be kept in mind that our question dealt specifically with the respondent's perception of the fit between his job and his "education and skill." See Robinson, J. P., Athanasiou, R., and Head, Kendra B., *Measures of Occupational Attitudes.* Ann Arbor, Michigan: Survey Research Center, 1969.

with employment does not vary from one race to the other once education is controlled. Negro college graduates may be somewhat more satisfied with their jobs than white college graduates are with theirs; otherwise
race does not seem to contribute anything unique to level of job satisfaction.

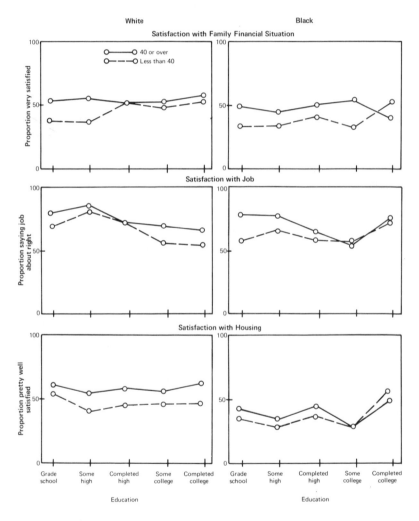

Figure IV-4. Relation of Satisfactions with Housing, Job and Family Financial
Situation to Level of Education

Satisfaction with housing does not vary by educational level but it does vary by race. Negroes at all age and educational levels (except one) are less satisfied with their housing than white people of the same levels. The one exception is the under-40 Negro college graduates who are at least as satisfied with their housing as young white college graduates.

If we carry out a similar analysis using occupation as a measure of achievement we find a pattern very similar to that shown in Figure IV-4. Satisfaction with income, job and housing does not increase as we move from the lower status positions, laborers and service workers, to the managers and professionals, although young Negro professionals stand out within their race. Housing is again seen to have a clear racial component with white people expressing greater satisfaction with their housing than Negroes of equal age and occupation. The one exception to this pattern is the young Negro professionals who are more satisfied with their housing than young white professionals.

Several observations emerge from this exploration into the relationship between achievement and satisfaction. In the first place we find it interesting that satisfaction with one's own financial situation increases as income increases. If economic aspiration were always a proportionate increase, say 10 percent, over one's present economic achievement we would not find such a relationship. Satisfaction levels would be the same at all income levels. But the fact that low income people are more dissatisfied than high income people must mean that high income *per se* has some motivating force throughout the income range. There seems to be some more or less common financial status to which Americans at all income levels aspire and the further they are away from it the less satisfied they are with what they have. The same may be said in lesser degree about housing; here again there seems to be a common standard which people of low income are further away from than people of higher income and are accordingly less satisfied.

It is also noteworthy that this relationship between income and satisfaction with financial situation is almost precisely the same for blacks as for whites. Black people apparently relate themselves to the same financial standard white people do. The fact that the average black income is much lower than the white average does not mean that black people are more satisfied with a low income than white people with that same income.

Secondly, we observe that while satisfaction with income and with occupational status does not appear to have any uniquely racial quality, satisfaction with housing clearly does. Satisfaction with housing increases with income in both races but Negroes are not as well satisfied with their housing as whites who have the same income they do. It is not surprising that urban Negroes as a group are less satisfied with their housing than urban whites; they have less to be satisfied with. The important fact is that when we rule out differences in income (as well as educational and occupational status) the discrepancy in satisfaction level remains. There may be various reasons for this discrepancy but one of them must have something to do with the relative difficulty an urban Negro has in upgrading his housing. Whereas Negro incomes have been going up, both in real wages and in relation to white levels, and Negro occupations have been improving, the ability of Negro ghetto dwellers to move into more satisfactory housing is severely restricted by the limitations on Negro housing which have existed historically in all of these cities. Thus a Negro family may feel relatively satisfied with its income or its occupational status because it has some sense of improvement over the years, but if this improvement is associated with an inability to upgrade one's housing, it is very likely that this housing will in due course become the subject of grievance.

The third point of interest in these data is the fact that neither educational level nor occupational status relates in any consistent way with level of satisfaction with financial situation, housing or job, a fact which is equally true of both races. Education is not very closely correlated with family income among these urban people and it is clear that educational level means something different than income level so far as satisfaction with these conditions of life is concerned. Previous research has shown that college people are more self-critical than people of lesser education and we may surmize that they set higher aspirations for themselves. [11] This may explain the fact that their satisfaction levels are no higher than average even though their incomes, housing and jobs generally are. It is particularly interesting that there is little relationship between occupational level and satisfaction with one's occupation. People in lower status occupations are about as likely to express satisfaction with their jobs ("considering their education and skill") as those in the positions of highest status. Apparently it is easier to compare one's financial situation to a more affluent one than it is to compare one's job to one of higher level.

Finally, we note again the generally high level of satisfaction found among Negroes of high income, educational and occupational status, especially those below 40 years of age. Unfortunately, the number of Negroes in these categories in our study is rather small and we must take account of the possibility of large errors due to sampling in this group.

---

[11]Gurin, G., Veroff, J. and Feld, Sheila, *Americans View Their Mental Health*. New York: Basic Books, 1960.

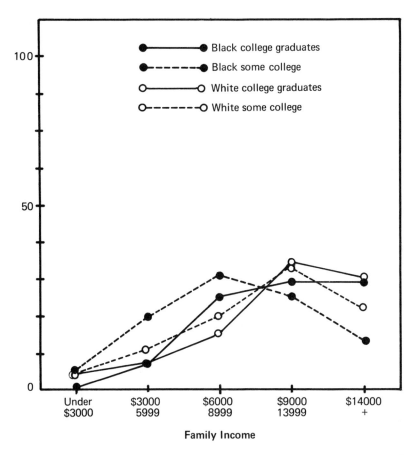

Figure IV-5. Annual Family Income of Blacks and Whites with Some and Complete College.

Nevertheless, the differences we see are large enough to suggest that the situation of high status Negroes is in some respect unique. When we compare the income distribution of Negro college graduates to that of the next lower category (some college) we find a much sharper increment than we do when we make the same comparison among white people (Figure IV-5). We also find that the distribution of incomes reported by these urban Negro college graduates does not differ greatly from that reported by white college graduates. These people, most of them under 40 years in age, are clearly more advantaged than the rest of the Negro population and they are financially better off than most of the white population. It is plausible to assume that their relatively high level of satisfaction comes from their recognition of this fact.

Conclusions

Quality of life is a concept which has at least two meanings. It is commonly used to refer to the objective conditions in which people live. One deplores the quality of the lives of people who are crowded into a deteriorated slum, working at poor pay at marginal jobs, subject to all the material inadequacies associated with poverty. In contrast, the lives of well-fed, well-housed, and well-cared for people of affluence may be thought to have a very different quality. The second sense of the concept of quality of life is psychological. One thinks in this case of terms like satisfaction, happiness, and fulfillment. People differ in the degree to which they believe their lives to be rewarding and satisfying.

There is a prevailing tendency among those who write about the quality of urban life to equate these two aspects of the concept. It is at least tacitly assumed that life without the comforts of middle-class affluence cannot be subjectively satisfying; that people living below this objective level must feel deprived and therefore unhappy. As Walter Miller has pointed out, middle-class students of the culture of poverty have developed a special vocabulary for the description of poverty which is replete with value judgments growing out of their own background, a vocabulary which is generally denigrative of the conditions of lower-class life. [12]

We doubt that the relationship between the objective conditions of life and the subjective experience of life is as simple as this formulation implies. That the objective circumstances of life of urban Negroes are on the average more modest than those of their white neighbors cannot be doubted. The evidence presented here simply specifies for the 15 cities of this study what is well-known for the country at large. Averages, of course, disguise great variability within each race, and the fact that there is a substantial Negro middle-class is often forgotten. Nevertheless, and despite the changes which have been taking place over the last 30 years, Negroes in the northern cities fall far short of the standard of living which white people in these cities have attained. That the experience of life

---

[12]Miller, Walter, *Bulletin of the American Academy of Arts and Sciences, 22,* 3, 1967, 15.

in these cities is less satisfying to black people than to white is also clear from the data we have reviewed in this chapter.

The important fact is, however, that most of the dissatisfactions which black people expressed in our interviews are not directly related to their economic, educational or occupational circumstances. In most of our measures of satisfaction with urban living we find consistent and sometimes substantial differences between races but not between people of different objective conditions within each race. Black people are more dissatisfied with the services they receive from their city than white people are but, with some exceptions, those of affluence and higher educational status are not characterized by higher satisfaction levels. Their dissatisfactions with these services appear to come more from their racial status than from any other consideration. Only satisfaction with family financial situation appears to be determined by the objective fact of income level, with no special reference to race. Satisfaction with housing is influenced by income level in both races but a substantial part of Negro dissatisfaction with housing remains when this influence is removed by comparing whites and blacks whose incomes are equal.

These findings lead us to ask whether the major differences in quality of life as it is experienced by whites and blacks in the cities derive from the economic and physical conditions of life of the two races or from considerations which are primarily psychological and social. We have seen something in this chapter of how whites and blacks see the community in which they live and it is apparent that in virtually every respect it is less satisfying to black people than to white. The perception of the police in particular reveals the great sense of discrimination and disadvantage which black people feel. Our evidence is not conclusive but it raises the question of whether the major source of discontent and protest among urban Negroes is primarily their below-average income, occupation and housing, or is instead the pattern of exclusion, subordination, and denigration which white society has traditionally assigned them.

V

THE RELATION OF WHITE ATTITUDES
TO DISSATISFACTION
AND POWERLESSNESS

The comparison of people at various locations in the social order makes clear that white attitudes toward race are found in full variety at every point we have looked. The pattern of racial attitudes in these 15 cities is a mixture and this mixture has a somewhat different configuration in different segments of the white population. Southerners who have moved to the northern cities continue to show the attitudes which are characteristic of their region of origin. The young college-educated generation has a positive orientation which sets it off from the rest of the population. Within each of the social locations we have examined, however, there are striking differences between individuals in their beliefs and attitudes regarding race. Even within those groups which depart most from the general pattern there are great differences in outlook and we must assume that they depend in large part on idiosyncratic factors of family background, personal experiences, or social relationships concerning which we have no information.

We must also take into account the fact that individual attitudes and behavior are to be understood not only in terms of their background in the life-history of the person, but also in terms of their relationship to the person's immediate psychological situation. We would not expect an individual who sees his world as secure, benign, and gratifying to feel the same about racial and other social issues as a person who feels himself surrounded by a threatening, unrewarding, and unresponsive environment. In other words, we assume that social attitudes will reflect in some degree the individual's perception of his psychological circumstances.

Satisfaction and Dissatisfaction

Social scientists have historically searched for explanations of inter-group attitudes and behavior in the frustrations growing out of unattained aspirations. The thesis that frustration predisposes to aggressive behavior has been tested in numerous analyses at both societal and individual levels.[1] A number of recent studies have undertaken to show that the current wave of black protest in this country is a reaction to a revolution of rising ex-pectations which has not been met by rising achievements. It may be reasonably assumed that white attitudes may also be influenced by a sense of deprivation or fulfillment.

We have seen in the preceding chapters a number of references to questions asking white people to express their satisfaction or dissatisfaction with certain aspects of their own personal situation and with various govern-mental and community activities. After examining the interrelationships of the responses to these various questions, we have developed three measures of satisfaction-dissatisfaction, as follows:

1. Satisfaction with economic circumstances, a com-bination of questions regarding family financial situation and housing;
2. Satisfaction with the mayor's efforts to solve city problems, a single question; and
3. Satisfaction with community services, a combina-tion of five questions regarding neighborhood schools, parks, teenage facilities, police protection, and garbage collection.

These three measures are not interrelated to the degree one might have expected. Reasonably enough, those people who complain that the local mayor's office is not working hard enough to solve the problems of their city are most likely to express dissatisfaction with the services they receive from the city but the relationship is a modest one (r=.16). The community services measure is similarly related to satisfaction with eco-nomic circumstances (r=.13) and the relationship between satisfaction with the mayor and satisfaction with economic circumstances is not sig-nificant (r=.06). Thus there is very little indication of a general attitude of satisfaction or dissatisfaction among these people; the three separate measures clearly have their own identity.

When we compare the racial attitudes of white people who place themselves on the satisfied and dissatisfied extremes of these three mea-

---

[1]Dollard, J., Doob, L. W., Miller, N. E., Mowrer, O. H., and Sears, R. R., *Frustration and Aggression.* New Haven, Conn.: Yale University Press, 1939.

sures we find very little meaningful difference. Our expectation that people who found these aspects of their life situation dissatisfying would be more inclined than average to negative attitudes regarding interracial contact, the prevalence of discrimination, and black protest activities is not supported. However, when we examine the attitudes of these people toward direct white aggression against Negroes, we find the kind of relationship our theory would have predicted; dissatisfaction is associated with hostility.

It is significant that dissatisfaction with community services is the most discriminating of the three dissatisfaction measures. We have divided the white population by educational level in Figure V-1 since we know that education plays an independent role in these racial measures and we see that low-education white people who are most dissatisfied with their neighborhood services are also most ready to condone anti-Negro violence. This relationship appears less dramatically among people who have graduated from high school and it disappears among college people, very few of whom approve of white rioting against Negroes. The measure of satisfaction with the mayor's efforts shows a similar but weaker relationship to attitudes toward white counterrioting. When we compare people who differ in degree of satisfaction with their income and housing (Figure V-1C) the pattern of relationships is less significant.

The measure of satisfaction with community services shows a further relationship to racial hostility when we relate it to the perception of dislike between the races. Figure V-2 shows the tendency of white people, especially those of low educational attainment, who are dissatisfied with their community services to see a great deal of dislike between whites and blacks. This figure has very much the same pattern as Figure V-1A and it suggests again that the perception of racial hostility is probably in part an expression of hostility. We find a similar relationship although not as strong when we compare people who are satisfied or dissatisfied with the quality of the mayor's action in their cities. Satisfaction with income and housing, on the other hand, seems unrelated to perception of racial hostility.

The data regarding satisfactions and attitudes leave several questions to be answered. First is the fact that our measures of satisfaction show no relationship to the three racial attitudes with which we have been concerned, but they are related to the more hostile expression of approval of white violence against Negroes. Insofar as we can feel confident in the validity of our measures of satisfaction we must conclude that white attitudes toward interracial contact, discrimination, and the black protest do not grow out of immediate dissatisfactions with the circumstances of life. These attitudes apparently develop as part of a general orientation toward race which the individual white person learns

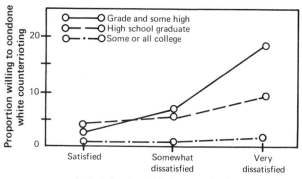

A. Satisfaction with Community Services

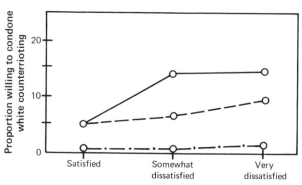

**B. Satisfaction with Mayor's Effort
to Solve City Problems**

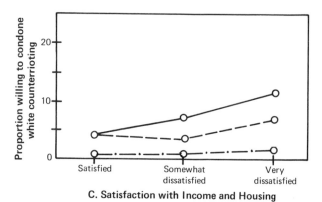

C. Satisfaction with Income and Housing

Figure V-1. Relation of Measures of Dissatisfaction to Willingness to Condone White Counterrioting

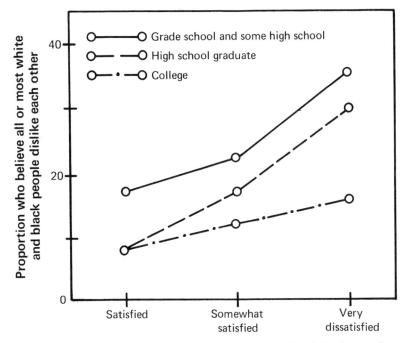

Figure V-2. Relation of Satisfaction with Neighborhood Services to Perception of Interracial Dislike

over his lifetime. None of them explicitly reflects hostility or dislike of black people *per se,* although as we have seen people whose attitudes are negative are much more likely to condone hostile acts by white people than are those who are positive in their outlook. The fact that willingness to see white violence against Negroes is associated with contemporary dissatisfactions suggests that this more aggressively hostile attitude is qualitatively different from the other measures. We might, for example, expect to see its incidence in the population oscillate according to the social stresses of the times, while the other attitudes might move more slowly in response to the long-term processes of education and socialization.

The second question which our data raise is why the measure of satisfaction with income and housing status is less closely associated with aggressive dispositions toward Negroes than the measures of satisfaction with community services are. The difference becomes reasonable if one assumes that satisfaction with income and housing grows out of one's personal aspirations and achievements, with relatively little relationship to the larger social context. These people apparently do not "understand their personal situation in social terms," to borrow Dudley Duncan's felicitous phrase.[2] Low income and poor housing may have some of the quality of poor health; it is not as easy to convert the frustration growing out of such a personal condition into aggression against society or any salient part of it as it would be if the frustration were with some aspect of society itself. Community services are obviously a direct function of society and must be perceived as such by everyone. The individual who is dissatisfied with these services has a grievance against society at large and this he may translate into aggression or resentment of any visible social scapegoat.

Finally we must ask why it is that the association between dissatisfaction and willingness to condone hostile acts toward Negroes is strongest among people with least formal education. There are two plausible explanations for this fact, both of which take into account the class differences between people of different educational levels. It is possible that these educational differences are entirely a matter of willingness to admit aggressive impulses to an interviewer; this may be easier for a person of modest education than for a person whom a college education has made more self-conscious. It is likely, however, that these differences go considerably beyond this; that people with little education are in fact more ready to displace their frustrations into aggressive acts than people with much. This is the hypothesis which the general literature regarding social class differences would support. College people, either coming from middle-class status or moving into it, would presumably have learned to inhibit direct physical aggression against other people and not condone it in others. We have seen earlier that college people taken as a whole are least likely to approve social aggression and we see now that their disapproval is not diminished by a sense of unhappiness about the functioning of their local community services.

Powerlessness

Theorists of motivation assert that "the tendency to act in a certain way depends on the expectancy that the act will be followed by a given consequence (or goal) and the value of that consequence (or goal) to the individual."[3] In other words, goal-directed activity is enhanced if the individual feels the goal is within his power to reach. If for reasons beyond

[2]Duncan, O. D., "Discrimination Against Negroes," *The Annals, 371,* 1967, 85-103.

[3]Atkinson, J. W., *Introduction to Motivation.* Princeton, N. J.: Van Nostrand, 1964.

his control the attainment of the goal appears to the individual to be blocked, his response may be expected to be one of frustration, or if the goal seems hopelessly unattainable, of passivity and lack of interest.

In recent years psychologists have undertaken to conceptualize an attribute of personality or of personal outlook variously referred to as sense of internal or external control, powerlessness, sense of personal efficacy, or other similar designations. All of these proposals assume that individuals are characterized in various degree by the belief that the world around them is subject to their control, that they are not helpless pawns of forces outside themselves which they have no power to influence. Various questionnaire forms have been developed intended to provide a measurement of this trait.

The Survey Research Center has for almost 20 years been interested in assessing the degree to which members of the electorate feel themselves to be effective participants in the electoral process and more recently this measure has been broadened to represent a general sense of personal efficacy. An adaptation of this measure was used in the questionnaires of this study of racial attitudes. The respondents, both white and black, were asked to describe themselves by responding to the following four sets of alternatives:

> *Have you usually felt pretty sure your life would work out the way you want it to, or have there been times when you haven't been sure about it?*

> *Do you think it's better to plan your life a good way ahead, or would you say life is too much a matter of luck to plan ahead very far?*

> *When you make plans ahead, do you usually get to carry out things the way you expected, or do things usually come up to make you change your plans?*

> *Some people feel they can run their lives pretty much the way they want to; others feel the problems of life are sometimes too big for them. Which one are you most like?*

By simply summing the number of "effective" answers given by each respondent we find the distributions shown in Table V-1.

As we see, urban white people score somewhat higher on this measure than black people in the cities, but this difference is small compared to those found within each race between people of different education and

TABLE V-1

Distributions of Sense of Personal Efficacy
(White and Black)

	WHITE	BLACK
No effective response	10%	16%
One	19	21
Two	25	25
Three	25	21
Four effective responses	21	16
Not ascertained	–	1
	100%	100%

income. Reasonably enough, the number of effective answers increases sharply with these two measures of personal achievement. There remain, however, extreme differences between individuals at the same educational and income levels in their responses to these questions.

Our interest in the measure of sense of personal efficacy is primarily in its relation to racial orientation. Our expectation is that people who feel themselves able to cope with the world around them will be more likely to respond positively to questions regarding race than will those who see themselves as having little power in the face of external forces. While there may be some among those of low efficacy who are apathetic and unmotivated, we assume that most of these people feel themselves blocked and frustrated from the attainment of their goals. We expect this sense of inability to overcome external obstacles to have the same psychological effects as the specific dissatisfactions we were concerned with in the preceding pages.

We discover, however, that we learn relatively little about the racial attitudes of white people when we compare those who rate themselves as effective to those who say they are ineffective. The relationships between the scale of efficacy and the various measures of racial outlook we have been using are generally inconsequential; feeling effective or ineffective apparently has little to do with how a white person feels about racial questions. There is one exception, sympathy with the black protest movement is a little higher among people who call themselves effective. The differences are not great but they still remain when the influence of income is controlled. Similarly, people with high scores of effectiveness are somewhat less likely to condone white violence against Negroes. When we relate our measure of sense of efficacy to the satisfaction measures we find that it has something in common only with the income-housing scale, not with the other two. The tendency of people who score themselves as effective to express satisfaction with their financial and housing situation is clear, however, and it is present at all educational levels. A similar pattern emerges when we group people by income instead of education; high efficacy is associated with high satisfaction with income and housing at all income levels.

It is evident from these data that sense of efficacy is independently related both to education and to satisfaction with income and housing. It is certainly not surprising that people of higher educational levels express a stronger sense of personal effectiveness; our confidence in the efficacy scale would be badly shaken if this were not true. The additional influence that satisfaction with income and housing appears to exert on sense of effectiveness must derive from the feeling of achievement a person experiences in attaining levels of income and housing he considers satisfactory. If he is disappointed and dissatisfied with his income and housing his sense of personal power is likely to be diminished. It is not easy for a person to feel responsible for the quality of his community services or for the activities of governmental agencies. He cannot take credit for them if they are satisfactory or feel personally inadequate if they are unsatisfactory. We have argued earlier that dissatisfaction with one's financial situation is not converted into social hostility for the reason that people do not typically interpret their financial fortunes or misfortunes in social terms. We assume that they do interpret them in personal terms and that this personal perception of success or failure has effects on the individual's sense of efficacy.

Previous research has shown that among Negroes a feeling of powerlessness is significantly associated with a greater willingness to use violence.[4] This association is not impressive in our white sample and in general our attempt to identify sense of personal efficacy as a source of individual differences in white attitudes toward race has proved unrewarding. There remains the possibility that feelings of inadequacy may interact with feelings of dissatisfaction to produce reactions which neither condition would produce by itself. Studies of Los Angeles Negroes have found the combination of high discontent and low efficacy to be most productive of inclinations to violence and conversely a combination of low

---

[4]Ransford, H. E., "Isolation, Powerlessness, and Violence," *American Journal of Sociology, 73,* 1968, 581-591.

discontent and high efficacy as least productive. Our data permit us to apply this same analysis pattern to a white population.

The consequence of this rather involved manipulation is negative. The "ideal types" of the Los Angeles study do not stand out in any distinctive way and there is no evidence that the combination of the two measures has isolated people peculiarly receptive or resistant to interracial hostility. The differences in attitudes associated with dissatisfactions remain, of course, but they are not sharpened by the additional refinement of dividing satisfied and dissatisfied people according to their answers to the scale of efficacy.

Conclusions

The data which we have reviewed in this chapter have not been dramatic. We have not been able to examine the function of dissatisfaction and feelings of ineffectiveness as fully as one would wish. Despite the limitations of our information, however, our analysis raises important questions regarding the nature of racial attitudes.

There seems little doubt that white people who are dissatisfied with their local community services and with their city government are more given to hostility toward Negroes than white people who describe themselves as satisfied. It is a matter of great interest, however, that this difference is not found in those attitudes and perceptions which do not reflect overt hostility. A white man who has a grievance against his community may convert this frustration into hostility toward a segment of that community. But this is not the mechanism which explains his general attitudes toward racial distance, his perception of racial discrimination, or in any important degree, his sympathy with the protest movement of black people. These responses appear to be independent of immediate dissatisfactions and frustrations; they must be aspects of a general racial orientation which has built up over the individual's lifetime.

Of course, we cannot be assured that the causal relationship we are suggesting, social dissatisfactions produce social hostility, is in fact real. There may be some third factor, a general embittered attitude toward society in general, for instance, which underlies both of these conditions. It would require a longitudinal study demonstrating that changes in satisfaction levels are followed by appropriate changes in hostility levels to establish the argument of causality. One can find some suggestion of such a relationship in the history of white aggression against Negroes in this country, the incidence of race riots during periods of war and postwar and the increase of lynching during periods of economic stress in the South, for example. But these are not critical tests and we regard our hypothesis of causation as plausible but unproved.

The fact that the measure of satisfaction with income and housing showed a weaker association with the expressions of hostility than did satisfaction with community services or local government raises the question as to whether dissatisfactions with one's personal circumstances are as readily translated into social aggression as dissatisfactions with some aspect of society itself would be. We have suggested that they probably are not, that poor income like poor health is likely to be seen as a personal misfortune that has no obvious social source. However, if one's financial misfortunes come to be identified with a broader economic catastrophe such as a national depression, they are likely to take on broader implication and we would expect a period of depression to be associated with heightened social hostilities.

Our attempt to find some further clue to the origin of individual differences in racial attitudes in the differences which exist among people in their sense of personal effectiveness has brought us nothing. One may be inclined to suspect that the simple four-item scale by which we undertook to measure this trait was not adequate to the task. We are not convinced that this is the answer. We are inclined to believe that it does measure sense of efficacy at least crudely and that this aspect of self-assessment simply does not contribute to the racial attitudes of white people. Here again we suspect that the ineffective white person tends to interpret his inadequacy and lack of power as his own personal misfortune rather than as the product of a malign or unjust society. A black person who feels himself powerless and ineffective may find it much easier to relate his personal situation to social causes.

Our study would obviously have profited from greater attention to the whole range of variables which might be identified as components of the individual personality. The studies of authoritarian personality have demonstrated a convincing relationship between the general trait of authoritarianism and attitudes toward ethnic minorities, and this work has subsequently been extended to explain attitudes toward Negroes specifically.[5] The explanatory variables we have used in this study leave much of the variance between individual attitudes unaccounted for and it would have been highly desirable to pursue this analysis further with the aid of personality measures.

---

[5] Adorno, T. W., Frenkel-Brunswik, E., Levinson, D. J., and Sanford, R. N., *The Authoritarian Personality.* New York: Harper, 1950.

VI

WHITE ATTITUDES
IN THE SUBURBS

The growth of the metropolitan suburbs since World War II has been one of the major components of population movement in this country during this period. While the proportion of the electorate living in these areas was near 20 percent in 1940, it is now estimated at close to 32 percent.[1]

The "flight to the suburbs" is not a movement which originated in the present problems of the cities. It is a contemporary expression of a circulation of populations which has been going on in most of these cities for over a hundred years. The movement toward the periphery by those national or cultural groups who were first on the scene, their place being taken by newer immigrant groups of limited economic means, is a familiar story. The replacement of whites by blacks in the inner cities undoubtedly has its own special characteristics, but the general pattern of movement is not a creation of our time.

In the earlier history of American cities the distinction between the out-migrants and the in-migrants was typically economic, often national origin, and sometimes religious. The unique quality of the present relationship of suburbs to central cities is racial and this is a difference having very far-reaching implications. The older citizens might have preferred to keep their outlying neighborhoods free of Irish, Poles, or Jews, but as

---

[1]Current Population Reports, Bureau of the Census, Series P-26, No. 415, January 31, 1969.

these newcomers achieved the economic ability to buy into previously exclusive areas, they inevitably did so and it was not possible to keep them out. The situation of black people is different. They are in the first place highly visible; it is impossible for a black family to move into a white neighborhood without attracting immediate attention. There is, in the second place, the long-established pattern of racial segregation which at one time covered almost all aspects of life and now still lingers on in the area of housing. And finally, there is the apprehension, distrust, and unease which many white people feel toward Negroes which makes it difficult, if not impossible, for them to accept normal relationships across racial lines. The consequence of all this is that it has been possible for the white populations on the periphery of the cities to keep black people out. Whether through restrictive covenants in sales agreements, informal exclusion by real estate agents and bankers, police intimidation, or vigilante activities on the part of white residents, many suburban areas have succeeded in remaining almost exclusively white.

These facts might well lead one to expect to find the white residents of the metropolitan suburbs unusually negative toward Negroes and unsympathetic toward their present pressure for racial equality. If we make the commonly expressed assumption that the major motivation impelling the white movement from the cities to the suburbs is to escape contact with black people this expectation might be strengthened. The reports of widespread arming of private citizens in some suburbs, of the provision by suburban police of target practice for frightened white women, of the formation of neighborhood "protection" societies all seem to lend substance to it.

We do not have in hand a full report of the attitudes of white people living in the suburbs of the 15 cities of our study. We did, however, take our white interview into the suburbs of Cleveland and Detroit and we are able to compare these people to those living within the city limits of the 15 cities. As we shall see, the picture of the belligerently racist white suburbanite which we have proposed turns out to be greatly overdrawn.[2]

White people in the suburbs are about as heterogenous as white people in the cities; they distribute differently on the major dimensions of social and economic status, but they are found at all levels. The most distinguishing feature of suburban white families (at least in Cleveland and Detroit) is their income; 58 percent report an annual income of over $10,000, while the corresponding figure in the cities is 34 percent. Their average educational level is somewhat higher, mainly because fewer of

---

[2]A description of the suburban samples is given in Appendix B.

them have had only a grade school education, eight percent as compared to seventeen percent in the cities. They are only slightly more likely to have attended college. Their occupations fall more commonly into the professional, sales, and skilled craftsmen categories, but here again the differences with city people are not remarkable. They are much more likely to live in detached single-family houses and to own the home in which they live. They typically occupy more space and their ratio of rooms to persons is higher even though their families are on the average larger. The head of a suburban white household is likely to be younger than the head of a white household in the city, and considerable more likely to have small children in his home. He is somewhat more likely to be a Protestant and less likely to be a Catholic or a Jew, but his church-attending habits are similar to those of white people in the cities.

Suburban people are generally pleased with the communities in which they live. They consistently express higher levels of satisfaction with the services they receive from their community than do city people. This is especially true of their public schools, with which 69 percent say they are generally satisfied (as opposed to 48 percent in the cities) and of their police, with whom 84 percent classify themselves as satisfied (as compared to 68 percent in the cities). They are more likely to believe they could get their city officials to do something if they had a serious complaint about service, 63 percent as compared to 46 percent.

White people in the suburbs are far less likely to report unpleasant experiences with their police than are white people in the cities. Table VI-1 compares the reports from these two populations and it is apparent that suburban people do not believe their police are guilty of the practices suggested in our interview and they very uncommonly assert that they themselves have been subjected to objectionable treatment. As we have seen earlier, white people generally are less likely to criticize the police than are black people, but suburban whites have particularly little complaint. One must be impressed by the indication from Table VI-1 of how careful the suburban police are about laying rough hands on their local white citizenry.

In contrast to their generally favorable reports regarding community services, the evaluations suburban people give of the private services they receive are not more or less positive than those offered by white people in the cities. When asked about stores and merchants in their neighborhood, suburban people complain of overcharging, inferior goods, and disrespectful service as least as often as city people do. People in the suburbs are obviously not indiscriminately favorable toward all aspects of suburban life.

Neither are they especially well-pleased with the economic circumstances of their lives. We have seen earlier that white and black people

TABLE VI-1

Experiences With Police Reported by
Suburban and Central City White People
(Proportions of total samples)

	Suburban	Central City
Believe police do not come quickly when called	14.0	27.0
Report this has happened to them	9.0	15.0
Believe police don't show respect	9.0	16.0
Report this has happened to them	3.0	7.0
Believe police search people without good reason	4.0	11.0
Report this has happened to them	0.6	3.0
Believe police rough up people unnecessarily	4.0	9.0
Report this has happened to them	0.2	1.2

in the cities do not differ very substantially in their satisfaction with their "family financial situation" even though their average income levels are quite different. We now find that the proportion of suburban people who classify themselves as "pretty well satisfied" with their financial status is precisely the same as that of city white people, although the latter are considerably less affluent. The same results appear when we compare satisfaction with the level of pay and responsibility city and suburban people feel in their jobs; the two populations do not differ. In housing there is a difference; suburban people are somewhat more likely to be "very satisfied" with the housing they now have, 61 percent as compared to 52 percent of city white families. Here again the findings parallel those of the white-black comparisons in the cities. Suburban people, whose incomes, jobs, and housing are all superior to those of city white people, appear to be no more happy about their incomes or jobs, but they are more pleased with their housing. Whether this satisfaction comes from the specific qualities of the structures in which these people live or from the neighborhood settings in which they are located we do not know, but it is evident that housing has a peculiar ability to create group differences in satisfaction in the populations we have been comparing.

When we come to examine the racial attitudes of white people in the suburbs, we find that for the most part they closely resemble those of white city people. We see in Table VI-2 how little difference there is in these populations in their positions on the three basic measures of racial attitudes with which we have been concerned; only in sympathy with the black protest is there a suggestion of a less positive reaction.

TABLE VI-2

Racial Attitudes of Suburban and City White People

	Suburban	City
Attitude Toward Interracial Contact		
1 Unfavorable	11%	10%
2	31	29
3	30	30
4	18	21
5 Favorable	7	6
Not ascertained	3	4
	100%	100%
Perception of Discrimination		
1 Low sensitivity	14%	16%
2	20	21
3	30	28
4	19	21
5 High sensitivity	11	9
Not ascertained	6	5
	100%	100%
Sympathy With Black Protest		
1 Low	10%	13%
2	19	26
3	29	23
4	23	20
5	13	12
6 High	6	6
	100%	100%

These resemblances continue when we look at the proposals for action which these people accept or reject. Like city people, they are generally accepting of civil rights legislation and of federal programs of aid to the cities. They are no more likely to believe that police control is the answer to the problem of urban violence or to condone the suggestion that white people should take to the streets in retaliation. They are, finally, neither more nor less likely than city people to believe that most white and black people dislike each other.

There is one point, however, at which the racial experiences of suburban and city white people differ markedly; suburbanites do not live in the same neighborhood with Negroes. While nearly half of the city white families report that they live within two or three blocks of a black family, only 11 percent of white families in the suburbs do. While 15 percent of city white people report knowing personally one or more Negro neighbors and 10 percent say they have friends among them, this type of association is rarely found in the suburbs. Although white suburbanites are no less likely than city people to report having had Negro friends outside their neighborhood, there are few Negro families in their residential areas and they do not know them as friends.

This isolation of white suburbanites from black people is not associated with an extraordinary wish among these people to avoid interracial contact. This is apparent from Table VI-2 where the distributions of answers given by suburban and city people to questions regarding such contact are given. Looking at these questions individually, we do see a slightly greater sensitivity to neighborhood integration among suburban people, 55 percent of whom say they would feel at least a little disturbed at the prospect of having a Negro family of similar status move next door while this figure is 44 percent among urban people. They are also a little more likely to defend the right of white people to keep Negroes out of their neighborhoods if they wish, the percentages in this case being 34 and 29. A slightly larger proportion of them say they or some member of their family have moved from a neighborhood because Negroes were moving in, 20 percent of the suburbanites and 15 percent of people in the cities. These differences are consistent, but they are not large. Considering their general outlook on racial questions more broadly it appears that suburban and city people differ very little.

Conclusions

The growth of the metropolitan suburbs during the past generation has been accompanied by a generous outpouring of volumes devoted to the

unique qualities of life in suburbia. The morals and manners of suburbanites have attracted much attention, typically with an emphasis on their
contrast with the more conventional ways of life in the central city. We
are not in a position to provide documentation of all the presumed pecu-
liarities of suburban people and particularly not of those special enclaves
which hold so much interest for commentators on the culture of the suburban belt. Our data are very restricted and they do not tell a very exotic
story.

Within the limits of our evidence we have the impression that white
people living around Cleveland and Detroit do not differ substantially from
those who live within the city limits. It is a fact that people of very low
income and very limited education are relatively infrequently found in
the suburbs and of course the suburban dweller is much more likely to
live in and own a single family home than is the city person. There are
other differences of age, religion, and occupational status, but none of
these differences seems large enough to justify thinking of suburban people
taken as a whole as qualitatively different from people in the city.

Whatever its other attributes, life in the suburbs seems to be distinguished by relatively high levels of satisfaction with the quality of
various community services. Suburban people are not particularly un-
complaining; they are as ready to criticize the service they receive from
their local merchants as city people are. It may be that the actual standards of public service are higher in the suburbs than they are in the city;
this is suggested by the reports of experiences with the police. Or it may
be that members of a relatively small community are more likely to be
satisfied with their public servants, simply because of a stronger identification with community which is possible in a smaller population. Whatever the cause, public services seem more satisfactory in the suburbs than
they do in the cities.

The suggestion that suburban people might be found to be particularly negative and hostile on questions of race proves to be almost entirely
misleading. The numerous comparisons we are able to make of the attitudes and perceptions of white people in the cities and in the suburbs
do not show any important difference. Suburban people are more likely
to live in all-white neighborhoods and they are somewhat more sensitive
to the prospect of having black people move into these neighborhoods.
Aside from this specific difference, which is not large, white people in the
cities and suburbs may be best described as sharing the common white
pattern of attitudes toward race.

VII

STABILITY AND CHANGE
IN RACIAL ATTITUDES: 1964-1970

The preceding chapters have reviewed the evidence from our 15 city survey describing the quality of white attitudes toward race. The interviews from which this evidence was drawn were taken in the early months of 1968 and the study represents the state of white attitudes at that point in time. We have offered some speculation as to the possible trends which may underly these 1968 attitudes but it has been apparent that a single measurement provides a poor basis for the assessment of change through time.

We are now able to draw on an additional set of survey data which give us a more convincing sense of the presence or absence of movement in these attitudes during the period surrounding our 1968 15 city study. In October 1964 the Survey Research Center put into the field a national survey of the presidential vote in which a sample of the electorate was interviewed regarding the political alternatives offered in the campaign of that year. Included in this interview was a series of questions relating to race; some of these questions were identical with those used in the 15 city study, most were different. In October 1968 and in November 1970 similar national surveys were undertaken by the Center, also based on representative samples of the electorate repeating the racial questions which had been asked in 1964. Thus we have in hand three measurements derived from identical questions and based on comparable samples of the national adult population. The number of racial questions asked in the three surveys was not extensive but because of their fortuitous timing they provide a before-and-after measurement of racial attitudes and experiences prior to and following the critical 1965 to 1968 period of racial violence in the nation's major cities.

The first of the three surveys, in October 1964, preceded by a few months the outbreak of the Watts riot. On August 11, 1965 a police arrest in the Watts area of Los Angeles led to a violent period of rioting, fire-bombing and looting which resulted in 34 deaths, hundreds of injuries and $35 million of property damage. In the words of the Kerner report:

> The Los Angeles riot, the worst in the United States since the Detroit riot of 1943, shocked all who had been confident that race relations were improving in the North and evoked a new mood in Negro ghettos across the country.

In 1966 events of a similar intensity but more restricted scope occurred in Chicago and the Hough area of Cleveland. In the Summer of 1967 riots of great violence broke out in Detroit and Newark and major disorders occurred in various other cities. In April 1968, following the assassination of Martin Luther King, violent reactions resulted in deaths and destruction in the ghettos of Washington, D. C., Baltimore and Philadelphia and lesser disturbances in other major cities. This proved to be the final act in the three-year sequence of urban riots; lesser disturbances continued to occur in the two years following but the period of major disorders in the cities had at least temporarily ended. Our second survey, in October 1968, came shortly after the close of this period and the third followed in November 1970 after two years of relative quiet.[1]

In order to assess the changes in attitudes, beliefs and perceptions which occurred during the period of the urban riots it is necessary to compare the measurements taken prior to the riot period to those taken after its termination. The questions with which we are concerned fall into five different categories. We will consider first a series of three questions which relate to different aspects of civil rights (employment practices, schooling, and public accommodations). We will then examine a group of questions which ask the respondent's personal views on racial segregation. There follow four questions relating to the respondent's reactions to the black protest of the preceding years. Two questions ask the respondent to place white and blacks on a "feeling" scale, a measure intended to record the warmth or coldness of personal feeling toward the two races. Finally,

---

[1]The selection of respondents in these surveys was based on the refined procedures of probability sampling employed by the Survey Research Center. In 1964 the sample included 1,399 white and 159 black respondents; in the 1968 sample there were 1,387 white and 149 black respondents; the 1970 sample was smaller, with 685 white and 147 black respondents.

we will review a series of seven questions which ask the respondent to report the amount of interracial contact he experiences in various social contexts.

Civil Rights

In asking opinions regarding civil rights it is possible to frame the question in terms of the abstract right itself or in terms of the political issue associated with it. Because the surveys in which the questions being reported here were asked were primarily concerned with political behavior we chose the latter format; the respondents were asked whether they thought the federal government should intervene in defense of the right in question or whether the government should stay out of the matter, leaving it to the states or local communities. This means, of course, that some of our respondents who might have supported the particular right on principle would object to the government's intervention because they believe such questions should be handled locally. In Table VII-1, for example, we see that only a third of the white sample support governmental enforcement of fair employment practices although we saw in Chapter II

TABLE VII-1

Attitudes Toward Governmental Policies
Regarding Fair Employment Practices

"Some people feel that if Negroes are not getting fair treatment in jobs the government in Washington ought to see to it that they do. How do you feel about it? Should the government in Washington see to it that Negroes get fair treatment in jobs or leave these matters to the states and local communities?"

| | WHITE | | BLACK | |
	1964	1968	1964	1968
See to it they get fair treatment	33%	33%	87%	84%
It depends	8	7	3	1
Leave to the states	44	46	5	9
Don't know	4	2	1	1
Not interested enough to have an opinion	11	12	4	5
	100%	100%	100%	100%

that two out of three urban white people support the principle of equal treatment for the two races on the job. The important aspect of Table VII-1 for our present interests, however, is the fact that no change occurred in the answers to this question among either white or black people over the 1964-1968 interval. This question was not asked in the 1970 survey.

A different finding appears when we examine the answers to a question regarding governmental concern with the problem of school desegregation (Table VII-2). Here again only a minority of the white sample support such action although other surveys have shown substantial majorities supporting various statements of the principle of school integration over the years since 1954. In this case we find a decline in white support for governmental intervention in the integration of the schools between 1964 and 1968 and a recovery in 1970 to a point slightly higher than the 1964 level. This movement is not substantial but it is not due to factors of chance. In contrast black support for governmental intervention in this problem rose

TABLE VII-2

Attitudes Toward Governmental Policies
Regarding School Integration

"Some people say that the government in Washington should see to it that white and Negro children are allowed to go to the same schools. Others claim this is not the government's business. Do you think the government in Washington should:

| | WHITE | | | BLACK | | |
	1964	1968	1970	1964	1968	1970
See to it that white and Negro children go to the same schools	38%	33%	41%	68%	84%	84%
It depends	7	7	10	4	3	3
Stay out of this area as it is none of its business"	42	48	36	12	6	7
Don't know	3	1	1	7	3	1
Not interested enough to have an opinion	10	11	12	9	4	5
	100%	100%	100%	100%	100%	100%

substantially over this period from an already high level of support in 1964 to a level which in 1968 and 1970 was comparable to that shown by black people for governmental guarantee of fair employment practices.

The third question regarding governmental policies on questions of civil rights dealt with the right of black people to "go to any hotel or restaurant they can afford, just like anybody else." The Civil Rights Act of 1964 had explicitly guaranteed this right and the question asked referred to the fact that the Congress had passed such a law. Although less than half of the white sample in 1964 agreed that the government should support the equal right of Negroes to public accommodations there was a substantial shift in response to this question in the ensuing years. In 1970 the proportion of white people who supported governmental protection of this right was twice as large as that who felt the government should "stay out of this matter." Negroes were of course far more supportive of governmental action in this regard, the proportion in each year running approximately nine out of ten.

TABLE VII-3

Attitudes Toward Governmental Policies
Regarding Public Accommodations

"As you may know, Congress passed a law that says that Negroes should have the right to go to any hotel or restaurant they can afford, just like anybody else. Some people feel that this is something the government in Washington should support. Others feel the government should stay out of this matter. Should the government support the right of Negroes:

| | WHITE | | | BLACK | | |
	1964	1968	1970	1964	1968	1970
To go to any hotel or restaurant they can afford	41%	48%	56%	88%	90%	93%
It depends	4	3	4	1	1	1
Stay out of this matter"	43	37	27	3	4	2
Don't know	2	2	1	0	0	0
Not interested enough to have an opinion	10	10	12	8	5	4
	100%	100%	100%	100%	100%	100%

While the answers to these three questions do not reveal a consistent pattern of movement between 1964 and 1970 in white attitudes toward the desirability of governmental action in support of the civil rights of black people, one must be impressed with the fact that they give no evidence of a general white "backlash" in response to the events of this period. The decline in support of school integration between 1964 and 1968 has interest in view of the controversy which had developed during these years, particularly over problems associated with so-called *de facto* segregation. Analysis of the data shows that this decline was not located in the South, as might have been imagined, but in the Northeast and Midwest and among people of higher than average formal education. However, by 1970 support of school integration had returned to its earlier level or beyond. As we will see in Table VII-14, white perception of racial integration in their local schools rose sharply throughout this six-year period. In contrast to white uncertainties regarding the implementation of the 1954 school integration decision, white acceptance of racial integration in places of public accommodation has steadily increased and in 1970 was clearly the majority view. White people were more aware of black people in public places in 1970 than they had been in 1964 and this experience was accompanied by a growing approval of the government's role in protecting their right to be there.

It is not surprising, of course, that support of these federal laws regarding civil rights is so much higher among black people than it is among white. The only change of any consequence in black attitudes over the six-year period was the increase in support of governmental guarantee of school integration which in 1970 approached the very high levels of support of laws regarding fair employment practices and open public accommodations.

Attitudes Toward Desegregation

At the time of our 1964 survey the Congress had not passed the Civil Rights Act of 1968 which put most of the nation's housing under open occupancy regulation. Our question regarding housing was phrased in terms of "rights" rather than governmental policy and we see in Table VII-4 that in all three of our surveys a majority of white people gave at least verbal support to the right of Negroes "to live wherever they can afford to, just like anybody else." It is also clear that this majority has been increasing since 1964. Answers to this question varied quite substantially by region, by age and by educational and economic status but the increase in white acceptance of the right of open housing was general across all of these segments of the population. Black response to the principle of open housing was very positive in 1964 and nearly unanimous in the later surveys.

TABLE VII-4

Attitudes Toward Negro Rights to Open Housing

"Which of these statements would you agree with: White people have a right to keep Negroes out of their neighborhoods if they want to, or Negroes have a right to live wherever they can afford to, just like anybody else?"

| | WHITE | | | BLACK | | |
	1964	1968	1970	1964	1968	1970
White people have a right to keep Negroes out	29%	24%	21%	2%	1%	2%
Negroes have a right to live wherever they can afford to	53	65	67	89	96	97
It depends, don't know	18	11	12	9	3	1
	100%	100%	100%	100%	100%	100%

In order to obtain a more general reaction to the question of desegregation the respondents in all three surveys were asked whether they were "in favor of desegregation, strict segregation, or something in between." This question was preceded by two questions asking their perceptions of the attitudes of whites and blacks regarding this issue, the first of which read "How many of the Negroes in this area would you say are in favor of desegregation?" The most striking finding from this question is the decline from 1964 to the later years in the proportion of whites and blacks who said they didn't know how Negroes felt about desegregation (Table VII-5). A similar decline in uncertainty appeared in white attitudes toward segregation (Table VII-6) and these shifts indicate an increasing sensitivity to interracial problems in both racial groups. It is not surprising perhaps that black respondents saw Negroes as more favorable to desegregation than did white; the number believing most Negroes are opposed to desegregation being very small indeed. Over the six-year period of our surveys, taking into account the variations in the proportions who did not

offer an opinion, we find a decline in the proportion of the white population who see all Negroes as favoring desegregation, a reaction perhaps to the
separatist doctrine they have heard expressed in recent years by some black
leaders. Most Negroes believe that most of the Negro population favors desegregation and this belief has not changed significantly over the period of
our surveys.

The question regarding perception of white attitudes reversed the
wording of the previous question and asked "how many white people in
this area are in favor of strict segregation of the races?" (Table VII-6).
Here again the large number of nonresponses creates ambiguities but if
they are removed we see that over the 1964-1970 period there has been
a significant decline in the number of white respondents who believe that
"all or most white people" favor strict segregation of the races. Black
perceptions of the attitudes of "white people in their area" did not change
significantly during this period, and in 1970 black estimates of the proportions of white people who were "strict segregationists" did not differ
significantly from those of white people themselves.

TABLE VII-5

Perceptions of Negro Attitudes Toward Desegregation

*"In general how many of the Negroes in this area would you say are in favor of de-
segregation?"*

| | WHITE | | | BLACK | | |
	1964	1968	1970	1964	1968	1970
All of them	11%	11%	6%	26%	27%	26%
Most of them	12	16	14	32	40	42
About half	6	13	13	11	13	21
Less than half, or	7	11	10	6	8	6
None of them	2	2	3	1	3	0
Don't know	30	10	13	19	7	4
Not ascertained	8	1	2	5	1	1
No Negroes in this area[a]	24	36	39	0	1	*
	100%	100%	100%	100%	100%	100%

[a]In 1968 and 1970 the alternative "No Negroes in the area" was printed on the
questionnaire; in 1964 it was not.

TABLE VII-6

Perceptions of White Attitudes Toward Strict Segregation

"How about white people in this area? How many would you say are in favor of strict segregation of the races . . . . . . ?"

	WHITE			BLACK		
	1964	1968	1970	1964	1968	1970
All of them	12%	9%	9%	3%	8%	7%
Most of them	23	34	18	18	22	20
About half	10	22	22	18	21	26
Less than half, or	12	20	29	20	26	20
None of them	3	4	6	8	5	10
Don't know	20	10	14	28	8	4
Not ascertained	20	1	2	3	0	1
No whites in the area[a]	0	*	*	2	10	12
	100%	100%	100%	100%	100%	100%

[a]In 1968 and 1970 the alternative "No whites in the area" was printed on the questionnaire; in 1964 it was not.

After these expressions of belief regarding the general attitudes of white and black people were obtained, the question was then directed to the individual respondent's own point of view. Table VII-7 demonstrates that the modal preference of white people is for something in between desegregation and strict segregation. The striking fact is, however, that there was a clear decline between 1964 and 1970 in the number of white people who called themselves strict segregationists. Such people are far more numerous in the South than they are elsewhere in the country but the decline in their numbers was considerably more marked in the South than in the other regions. Other relatively segregationist segments of the population also moved toward desegregationist views (low income, low education, farmers) but older people (over 60) who are more segregationist than any of the younger decades remained unmoved while the younger generations shifted toward desegregation.

Black people are far more likely to favor desegregation than are white and their views changed little in the six-year period. A very small minority call themselves strict segregationists but it is interesting that in the face of a good deal of separatist thought among some sections of the black community this minority became, if anything, even smaller.

TABLE VII-7

Attitudes Toward Desegregation

"What about you? Are you in favor of desegregation, strict segregation, or something in between?"

	WHITE			BLACK		
	1964	1968	1970	1964	1968	1970
Desegregation	27%	31%	35%	72%	72%	78%
Something in between	46	48	44	20	19	19
Strict segregation	24	16	17	6	5	3
Don't know	3	5	4	2	4	*
	100%	100%	100%	100%	100%	100%

Attitudes Toward the Black Protest

As we have noted, the years between 1964 and 1968 were a period of great upheaval in the Negro community, including many forms of protest of which the most dramatic were the great urban riots. That these events and their implications should be seen differently through white and black eyes is obviously to be expected and it would not be surprising if they had an effect on attitudes toward the overall civil rights movement. The first of these expectations is amply confirmed by the evidence of our surveys and changes in attitudes did indeed occur between 1964 and 1970 among both whites and blacks.

White assessment of the impact of the civil rights movement in improving the situation of the Negro gradually increased over the six-year period (Table VII-8), with over half of the white sample in 1970 believing that there had been "a lot of change in the past few years." Black evaluation of how much "real change" had occurred followed a different pattern. In 1964 and 1968 well over half of the black respondents felt that "a lot of change" had taken place; in 1970 this proportion had fallen off to 41 percent. The meaning of this drop becomes clearer when we associate it with other changes we will see in black attitudes.

The increase in white perception of change was rather evenly distributed over the population, except in the metropolitan areas where this perception was high in 1964 and remained so in later years. Sensitivity to these changes was higher in the South than in the other regions of the nation and these regional differences were even greater in 1968 and 1970 than they had been in the earlier survey.

TABLE VII-8

Perceptions of Change in Position of the Negro

"In the past few years we've heard a lot about civil rights groups working to improve the position of the Negro in this country. How much real change do you think there has been in the position of the Negro in the past few years: a lot, some or not much at all?"

| | WHITE | | | BLACK | | |
	1964	1968	1970	1964	1968	1970
A lot	38%	49%	54%	57%	61%	41%
Some	39	35	33	31	32	45
Not much at all	20	15	10	11	6	14
Don't know	3	1	3	1	1	0
	100%	100%	100%	100%	100%	100%

Most white people felt in 1964 that the "civil rights people have been trying to move too fast" (Table VII-9). This proportion had not changed in 1968 immediately after the urban riots but it declined in 1970, apparently reflecting the period of relative calm in the intervening years. In contrast 10 percent or less of the black population believed their leaders were pushing too fast and an increasing proportion of them felt they are moving too slowly. Table VII-9 provides a second indication of a growing dissatisfaction among black people, particularly during the 1968-1970 period, with the progress they saw their race achieving.

There are substantial differences between the races in the extent to which they see the Negro protest as having been mainly violent (Table VII-10). Both whites and blacks were more likely in 1968 to say that most Negro actions in the preceding year or so had been violent than they had been in 1964, a reflection one may assume of the civil disorders prior to 1968. But in 1970 the labeling of Negro protests as violent had receded in both races.

TABLE VII-9

Attitudes Toward Speed of Movement
of Civil Rights Leaders

"Some say the civil rights people have been trying to move too fast. Others feel they haven't pushed fast enough. How about you, do you think that the civil rights leaders are trying to push too fast, are going too slowly, or are they moving at about the right speed?"

| | WHITE | | | BLACK | | |
	1964	1968	1970	1964	1968	1970
Too fast	68%	68%	57%	10%	6%	7%
About right	21	23	30	62	62	52
Too slowly	3	4	6	23	28	39
Don't know	8	5	7	5	4	2
	100%	100%	100%	100%	100%	100%

TABLE VII-10

Perceptions of Violence in Civil Rights Actions

"During the past year or so, would you say that most of the actions Negroes have taken to get the things they want have been violent, or have most of these actions been peaceful?"

| | WHITE | | | BLACK | | |
	1964	1968	1970	1964	1968	1970
Most have been violent	61%	73%	61%	18%	26%	25%
Some violent, some peaceful	4	3	3	6	7	3
Most have been peaceful	23	17	25	64	58	61
Don't know	12	7	11	12	9	11
	100%	100%	100%	100%	100%	100%

Two-thirds of the white population believed in 1968 that Negro actions in pressing for civil rights had on the whole hurt their cause rather than helped it (Table VII-11). This proportion was only slightly higher than it had been in 1964. Black people saw the situation in precisely opposite terms, two out of three of them saying in 1968 that on the whole Negro actions had helped their cause, a slight decline from the proportion making this statement in 1964. In 1970 both races were somewhat more willing than they had been in 1968 to accept Negro actions as "on the whole" helpful but the differences between white and black evaluation of their helpfulness remained very large.

TABLE VII-11

Attitudes Toward Effect of Civil Rights Action
on Negro Cause

"Do you think the actions Negroes have taken have on the whole helped their cause, or on the whole have hurt their cause?"

| | WHITE | | | BLACK | | |
	1964	1968	1970	1964	1968	1970
Helped	21%	21%	25%	72%	66%	78%
Both helped and hurt	4	3	4	1	7	3
Hurt	63	69	62	14	16	11
Don't know	12	7	9	13	11	8
	100%	100%	100%	100%	100%	100%

White response to the black protest movement, as shown by the answers to these questions was generally unfavorable, a majority believing it to be pushing too fast and too violently and with hurtful consequences. These attitudes did not develop during the 1964-1968 period; they were present in 1964 and changed rather little during the years of urban violence. They appear to have ameliorated somewhat during the more quiet years between 1968 and 1970.

Black evaluation of the black protest was far more positive than that of whites but black satisfaction with the pace of the civil rights movement and the amount of "real change" achieved declined perceptibly in 1970 from the level of the two earlier surveys. We may speculate that this reflected a rising level of aspiration among black people or a disappointment growing out of the failure to fulfill aspirations which were raised during the period of the urban riots. In any case, it is evident that in 1970 white people were more likely to perceive significant improvement in the Negro condition than were Negroes themselves.

Feelings Toward Whites and Negroes

If white and black people are pulling away from each other, moving toward two societies as the Kerner Commission concludes, we should expect to find increasing evidence of coolness and dislike between the races. Individual cases of this kind undoubtedly occur but the important question is whether collective changes in feeling regarding the other race are taking place.

The three surveys from which we are drawing data utilized an elaborate "feeling thermometer" device to ascertain the degree of warmth or coolness the respondents felt toward various segments of the population (farmers, liberals, Catholics, labor unions, whites, Negroes, etc.). We see in Table VII-12 how these white and black respondents placed themselves on this "thermometer" in indicating their feeling toward whites.

White people, naturally enough, placed themselves for the most part on the warm or favorable side of the thermometer with the modal position being the 100 degree or most favorable category (Table VII-12). Black people were much less favorably disposed, although only about 10 percent classified their feelings toward white people as unfavorable. White feeling toward white people shaded off gradually between 1964 and 1970; the major change being a drop in the number who classified their feelings in the most favorable category. The meaning of this deterioration in the quality of white self-regard is not immediately apparent; whether it reflects white reaction to the growing criticism of white racial practices or to some other aspect of the current national discontent we have no way of knowing. Black feeling toward whites also cooled somewhat during this period; Table VII-12 shows a general shift downward in the distribution of feelings expressed. The shift is not massive but it is sufficient to suggest a somewhat more critical quality in the collective black view of white people than had existed six years earlier.

White feelings toward black people are far less favorable than their feelings toward their own race. The proportion of white people who classify

TABLE VII-12

Feelings Toward Whites and Negroes

"There are many groups in America that try to get the government or the American people to see things more their way. We would like to get your feelings toward some of these groups. Where would you put whites on the feeling scale?"

	WHITE			BLACK		
	1964	1968	1970	1964	1968	1970
Zero, very unfavorable	0%	0%	*%	5%	5%	3%
Quite unfavorable	*	*	*	1	0	0
Fairly unfavorable	*	0	0	1	3	4
Slightly unfavorable	*	*	*	1	5	5
50, no feeling either way, neutral	10	15	17	31	15	22
Slightly favorable	4	4	9	11	9	15
Fairly favorable	12	16	15	10	22	18
Quite favorable	21	23	26	16	21	16
100, very favorable	51	39	30	22	16	14
Don't know, not ascertained	2	3	3	2	4	3
	100%	100%	100%	100%	100%	100%

"Where would you put Negroes on the feeling scale?"

	WHITE			BLACK		
	1964	1968	1970	1964	1968	1970
Zero, very unfavorable	3%	2%	5%	0%	0%	1%
Quite unfavorable	2	3	3	0	0	1
Fairly unfavorable	4	3	4	0	0	1
Slightly unfavorable	7	4	6	1	*	2
50, no feeling either way, neutral	28	30	34	4	3	4
Slightly favorable	13	15	15	3	3	3
Fairly favorable	21	20	13	8	6	7
Quite favorable	12	12	11	17	19	17
100, very favorable	8	8	5	65	65	63
Don't know, not ascertained	2	3	4	2	4	1
	100%	100%	100%	100%	100%	100%

themselves as unfavorable to blacks in some degree is quite small and it is not very different from the proportion of black people who express a negative feeling toward whites. Over a quarter said they had no feelings one way or another about black people. In their turn, black people are very much more positive toward their own race than they are toward white people and indeed than white people are toward the white race. Two-thirds of them placed the black race at the top category of the feeling scale and very few described themselves as having no feeling either way about black people. The important fact about Table VII-12 is the absence of movement from 1964 to 1968 and 1970. Despite the racial upheaval throughout the country during this period the evidence of cooling of feelings between the races seems relatively slight.

Reported Interracial Contact

It would be very difficult to estimate from the various offsetting changes in racial integration and segregation which are occurring in the present period whether the total net result in amount of interracial contact is increasing or declining. School enrollment figures show a substantial increase in the proportion of black children in the South who attend school with white children but in many large cities of the North *de facto* segregation of neighborhoods has increased the number of all-black schools. Federal and local legislation has opened up housing opportunities for black people but the white flight to the suburbs has increased the segregation ratio in the central cities. The diffusion of black people into occupational situations which they were earlier denied presumably has increased contact with white people on the job but the great increase in the size of Negro communities in the cities is creating all-black enclaves in which it is possible for black people to live, work, and shop with virtually no contact with white people.

There is no precise way of counting the points of contact between white and black people but it is possible to ask people of each race how much contact they have with the other race in various domains of their lives. Their estimates may be hardly more than impressionistic but when given at succeeding points in time they provide a measure of change in perceived racial contact. The first of the several questions regarding contact which our surveys asked had to do with the racial composition of the neighborhood in which the respondent lived (Table VII-13).

As we see, most white people report that they live in all white neighborhoods; very few see their neighborhoods as less than "mostly white." By contrast, only a quarter of black people see their neighbor-

TABLE VII-13

Perceptions of Neighborhood Racial Composition

"Is this neighborhood you now live in all white, mostly white, about half and half, mostly Negro, or all Negro?"

| | WHITE | | | BLACK | | |
	1964	1968	1970	1964	1968	1970
All white	80%	75%	73%	3%	1%	0%
Mostly white	16	19	21	7	15	15
Half and half	3	4	3	18	21	23
Mostly Negro	1	1	1	38	43	39
All Negro	0	0	0	33	19	22
Don't know	0	1	2	1	1	1
	100%	100%	100%	100%	100%	100%

hoods as all black and over a third report living in areas which are at least half white. In view of the fact that whites outnumber blacks some nine to one in this country it is not surprising that we find differences of this order. The less predictable fact which Table VII-13 reveals is the decline between 1964 and 1968 in the proportion of both races who see their neighborhood as totally segregated. Despite the indications of increasing separation of the races in the metropolitan centers, on a national basis the trend is in the opposite direction, at least in the perception of the population. The changes between 1968 and 1970 are consistent with this trend but are not large enough to be significant.

The integration of the schools has been the center of a confused and sometimes violent discussion ever since the 1954 decision of the Supreme Court. Community decisions, court directives and population movements have produced conflicting trends which make it impossible to plot precisely the net change in the extent of school integration. There is no doubt in the minds of the respondents of our surveys, however, as to what the total effect of these changes is; they see their schools becoming more integrated. Between 1964 and 1970 the proportion of white people who reported the grade school nearest them as being "all white" fell from 59 to 36 percent (Table VII-14). Declines of similar magnitude were reported for the nearest junior high school and high school. Correspondingly black people were less likely in 1970 to see their local schools as all black; over this six-year period this proportion fell from over a third to scarcely more than a tenth.

TABLE VII-14

Perceptions of Racial Composition of Nearest Schools

"Is the school nearest you . . . . . . ?"

	WHITE 1964	1968	1970	BLACK 1964	1968	1970
			Grade School			
All white	59%	36%	36%	4%	1%	1%
Mostly white	30	47	44	8	15	17
Half and half	2	5	7	9	19	23
Mostly Negro	2	2	3	23	34	36
All Negro	0	*	0	40	17	13
Don't know	7	10	10	16	14	10
	100%	100%	100%	100%	100%	100%
			Junior High School			
All white	47%	29%	25%	5%	0%	0%
Mostly white	33	46	45	8	14	15
Half and half	3	6	8	7	15	25
Mostly Negro	1	2	2	20	30	35
All Negro	*	*	0	37	14	12
Don't know or no junior high	16	17	20	23	27	13
	100%	100%	100%	100%	100%	100%
			High School			
All white	43%	27%	22%	5%	1%	0%
Mostly white	40	52	49	10	13	19
Half and half	4	7	11	9	18	28
Mostly Negro	1	2	3	20	34	33
All Negro	0	*	*	36	15	8
Don't know	12	12	15	20	19	12
	100%	100%	100%	100%	100%	100%

It will be noted that our surveys did not ask the respondents about the schools their own children attended and it would be hazardous to attempt to extrapolate from these tables an estimate of how many children attend schools of various degrees of integration. It is clear, however, that in the beliefs of white and black people there was significantly more school integration in 1970 than there had been six years earlier.

The work situation is one of the major areas of experience in which people of different racial origins come in contact. Our surveys tell us nothing about the nature of this contact but they give an indication of how commonly it occurs. It is inevitable that some 90 percent of the white respondents say the people where they work are mostly white (Table VII-15); it would have been more difficult to predict that something near half of the black respondents also work in mostly white situations. The proportion of white people who described their work group as "all white" declined between 1964 and 1968, a change which might have been anticipated from the fact that black job opportunities have been broadening. However, there was a small reversal of this movement in 1970, a reversal which we would not have predicted and which may result entirely from sampling error. The greatest change in the black reports is in the number who work in all white situations, a decline which may reflect the presence of multiple black workers in situations where there had previously been only one. The proportions who report working in all black situations is small, approximately one in ten, and remained small over the 1964 to 1970 period.

TABLE VII-15

Perceived Racial Composition of Place of Work

"Are the people where you work . . . . . . ?"

| | WHITE | | | BLACK | | |
	1964	1968	1970	1970	1968	1970
All white	54%	42%	47%	18%	9%	10%
Mostly white	39	45	41	35	30	32
Half and half	5	9	6	23	27	30
Mostly Negro	2	2	3	12	18	12
All Negro	0	0	0	11	11	9
Not ascertained	0	2	3	1	5	7
	100%	100%	100%	100%	100%	100%

The places where people "shop and trade" are the most racially mixed of the situations our surveys inquired about. Fewer than half (40 percent) of the white sample in 1964 said they shopped in exclusively white places and this proportion fell off sharply in 1968 to 25 percent (Table VII-16). Very few black people say they shop in all black places. The table of black shoppers shows the same characteristics as that of black workers. Apparently black people were less likely to find themselves the only black shopper in a white store in 1968 than in 1964 but white shoppers were no more likely to take their trade to all black establishments. The increase in the mixed character of shopping facilities between 1964 and 1968 was not extended further in 1970; the level reached in 1968 remained steady in 1970.

TABLE VII-16

Perceived Racial Composition of Shopping Place

"Are the people where you shop and trade . . . . . . ?"

| | WHITE | | | BLACK | | |
	1964	1968	1970	1964	1968	1970
All white	40%	25%	27%	15%	5%	6%
Mostly white	54	60	58	26	26	27
Half and half	5	13	12	44	51	52
Mostly Negro	*	1	1	11	11	13
All Negro	0	*	0	3	3	1
Don't know	1	1	2	1	4	1
	100%	100%	100%	100%	100%	100%

The final question of this series asked the respondents about their friends and Table VII-17 reveals the very great degree to which friendships in the United States are confined within racial lines. The great majority of white people say all their friends are white; black people are much more likely to report cross-racial friends but most of them report most or all of their friends as black. This demonstration of racial separation is impressive but at least as impressive is the fact that the number of people of both races who count their friends exclusively within their own race has declined over the past six years. This movement may have reversed in the black population in 1970; however, the small shift noted is well within the range of sampling error. Among white people the possession of black friends is clearly associated with higher educational and economic status, urban residence and youth. However, the increase in the number of white people reporting black friends is not located uniquely in any demographic segment but occurred generally throughout the population.

TABLE VII-17

Perceived Racial Composition of Friends

"Are your friends . . . . . . ?"

	WHITE			BLACK		
	1964	1968	1970	1964	1968	1970
All white	81%	70%	66%	0%	*%	0%
Mostly white	17	28	31	4	3	3
Half and half	1	2	2	24	17	23
Mostly Negro	0	*	0	30	54	45
All Negro	0	0	0	40	23	28
Not ascertained	1	*	1	2	3	1
	100%	100%	100%	100%	100%	100%

Patterns of Change

The foregoing tables make it clear that changes in racial attitudes, both black and white, occurred during the six-year period spanned by our surveys. The black components of our samples were not large enough to to give reliable indications of where within the black population these changes occurred but we can identify those parts of the white population which moved or remained stable between 1964 and 1970. We have noted specific instances of change in the preceding pages and we consider now the general patterns of change which appear in white attitudes between these four years.

The fact that the collective attitudes of a population become more favorable over a period of time presumably reflects the presence of some event or influence which affects more people positively than are affected negatively during that time period. Under some circumstances this net movement may occur more or less equally throughout the various strata of the population; that is to say, all parts of the population move in a positive direction from whatever their original attitude position was. In the election of 1952, for example, virtually every subdivision of the electorate was more Republican in its presidential preference than it had been in 1948. Those groups which had been most Democratic were still most Democratic and those which had been Republican remained Republican but they were all more Republican than they had been four years earlier.[2] A movement of this kind displaces the entire population in a common and more or less equal way and must result from influences which are not specific to particular groups but common to the whole population.

It may happen, however, that the influences which create attitude change over a period of time may affect different segments of the population quite differently. In 1960 Catholic voters moved to the Democratic presidential nominee in unprecedented numbers but in the South Fundamentalist Protestants swung strongly to the Republican candidate.[3] Those offsetting movements had the effect of widening the differences in the political attitudes of these two parts of the electorate. There may also be movements which decrease the amount of intergroup difference. Over a period of time discrepancies in the attitude of different groups may decline as the entire population moves toward a common position. We know, for example, that five years ago Medicare was more popular with retirement-age people than it was with younger people; it seems likely that this discrepancy has closed as Medicare has become an accepted piece of federal legislation.

When we examine the data from our three surveys to identify the pattern of the attitudinal changes we have recorded we find that although there are instances of both widening change and closing change the general pattern which emerges from the total array of data is one of common change. Our surveys provide far too many tables to reproduce here but it is possible to indicate in a selection of figures the pattern of common change which recurs so frequently. In Figure VII-1 we see that attitudes toward the principle of open housing differ rather substantially among

---

[2]See Campbell, A., Gurin, G., and Miller, W. E., "Political Issues and the Vote: November 1952," *American Political Science Quarterly, 47,* June 1953.

[3]See Converse, P. E., "Religion and Politics: the 1960 Election," in Campbell, A. *et al., Elections and the Political Order.* New York: John Wiley & Sons, Inc., 1966, 96-124.

white people of different age and education and in less degree among those in urban and rural settings but we also note that the increase in approval of open housing between 1964 and the later years was remarkably constant in all these subgroups of the population. A similar picture appears in Figure VII-2 which records the proportions of white people who say they have Negro friends. Here again there are differences by age, education and place of residence but in every category of these variables there is an increase in these proportions after 1964.

Figure VII-3 presents one of the few examples our surveys provide of a change which widened differences between population groups. Approval of public accommodation rights for Negroes was clearly related to educational level in 1964 but this relationship was even stronger in 1968 and stronger yet in 1970. The difference between the attitudes of white people of low education and those of college level increased over this period. Figures VII-4 and 5 give two examples of closing change. The South changed much more than the other regions in the proportion of whites who called themselves "strict segregationists" and the difference between the regions narrowed between 1964 and 1970. In 1964 the perception of "a lot of change" in the situation of Negroes was stronger in the metropolitan areas than it was in smaller communities but in 1968 and 1970 this difference was no longer present.

The general pattern of common change which dominates our data implies strongly that the forces which are producing change in white attitudes in the current era transcend the specific circumstances of particular population groups. Despite popular beliefs that this or that segment of the population is becoming more negative in its racial outlook in reaction to contemporary events we find no instances in which a specific group moves in opposition to a general positive change in the larger population. We see some cases in which a group which was negative to start with remains negative while the rest of the population becomes more positive (as in Figure VII-3) but even this is unusual. Perhaps if we could decompose our sample into smaller, more homogeneous groups we might find groups which are moving against the current. The important fact is that there is a current and that most of the population segments we are able to identify are moving with it.

Our surveys do not provide an answer to the question of what the forces which lie behind this general shift in white attitudes are. The six-year period is too short for any significant replacement of population; most of the change we see occurred among people who were members of the adult population in both 1964 and 1970. Although we do not have directly comparable data from years prior to 1964 the evidence which does exist from the last 25 years leads us to believe that the six-year period of

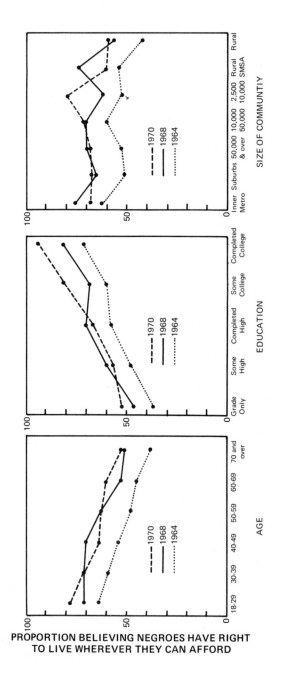

Figure VII-1. Changes in Attitudes of White People Toward the Principle of Open Housing by Age, Education and Size of Community

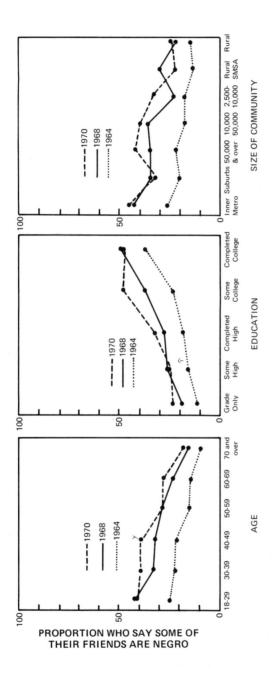

Figure VII-2. Changes in Proportions of White People Having Negro Friends by Age, Education and Size of Community

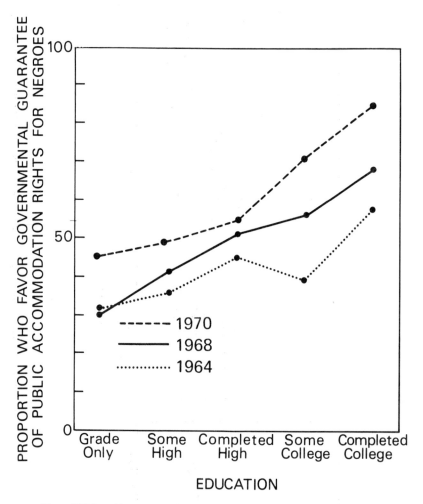

Figure VII-3. Changes in White Support of Public Accommodation Rights by Educational Level

our observation fits into a longer term trend which has seen a gradual erosion of the conventional beliefs in white superiority and racial segregation toward the conflicted mixture of racial attitudes we find in the white population at the present time.

ERRATA SHEET

PUBLICATION: WHITE ATTITUDES TOWARD BLACK PEOPLE

PAGE 153, FIGURE VIII - 4, BOTTOM GRAPH
ENTITLED "SIZE OF COMMUNITY," THE KEY
CODE IS TO BE CORRECTED AS FOLLOWS:

--------- 1970
————— 1968
.... 1964

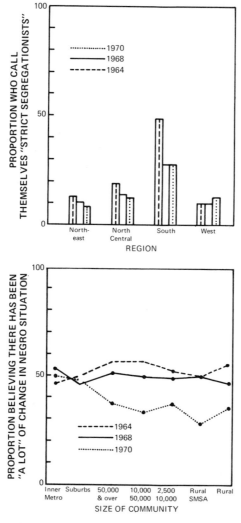

Figure VII-4. Changes in Proportions of White Population Perceiving a Lot of Change by Size of Community; Changes in Proportions of White Population Calling Themselves Strict Segregationists by Region

Conclusions

Between 1964 and 1970 there were many public evidences of strong polarity in the racial attitudes of individual Americans. The nationwide support given Governor George Wallace in the 1968 election demonstrated the fact that millions of white people were willing to support an overtly segregationist candidate and survey evidence makes it clear that many of them held highly segregationist attitudes.[4] Numerous instances of white resistance to change in segregation practices in schools and neighborhoods dotted the daily press. On the black side were the frankly antiwhite rhetoric of some of the militant leadership and the movement toward racial separation in some segments of the black population. Quite aside from the major acts of violence during this period there was ample reason to believe that there was dislike and distrust on both sides of the racial line.

The question with which we are here concerned is whether the collective attitudes of whites and blacks became more polarized over these six years; whether, as the Kerner Commission believed, the nation was moving toward two separate societies. It is impossible to conclude from the evidence we have reviewed that this is true. Our inquiry was limited and one may think of more penetrating questions that might have been asked but the data at hand had the great virtue of closely bracketing the riot period 1965-1968 and they do not show that the events of this period brought about a deterioration or widening of relationships between the races. On the contrary, within its limits, the evidence shows that on many questions of principle and policy white and black attitudes moved closer together. General measures of feeling toward the other race showed no dramatic change. Reports of cross-racial contacts in various social settings consistently showed increased contact and specifically increased contact as friends. It cannot be doubted, of course, that many white and black individuals moved away from each other during this period, both in attitudes and behavior, and the total number of such people may have been sizable. When the total population is considered, however, we find that such movement was fully offset by change of the opposite kind and that considered collectively the white and black populations have not moved farther apart.

There are indications in the 1970 survey of an increasing impatience among black people with the pace and accomplishments of the movement for racial equality. While this does not appear to have been translated into a growing hostility toward the white population it seems inevitable that if this frustration becomes more intense it will have implications for black-white relationships. Our national surveys give us no explanatory data which might illuminate the character of the 1970 shift and we can only speculate as to what it may foreshadow.

---

[4]Converse, Philip E., Miller, Warren E., Rusk, Jerrold G., and Wolfe, Arthur C., "Continuity and Change in American Politics: Parties and Issues in the 1968 Election," *The American Political Science Review LXIII,* December 1969, 1083-1105.

VIII

THE PRESENT
AND THE FUTURE

The racial situation in the United States defies understanding. The complexity and variety of the relationships between members of the two major races is so great that both white people and black tend to rely on simple generalities which reduce the problem to manageable terms. At the worst this degenerates into a crude form of racism, with blanket stereotyping of each race and naive beliefs about racial superiority. At the least it leads one to forget that the diversity within each race is far greater than the differences between races and that no characteristic is held universally within either.

The Quality of White Attitudes

The rhetoric of racial confrontation has recently leaned heavily on the concept of white racism and the United States is described by many as a racist society. In declaring that "white racism is essentially responsible for the explosive mixture" in the nation's cities the Kerner Commission went considerably further than any earlier federal document in labeling prevailing white attitudes and the label has been employed for more purposes than the Commission probably anticipated when it coined the statement.

It would certainly not have been necessary to conduct any research of the kind reported in this volume to demonstrate that racist attitudes are commonplace among white Americans. There is no need to document the obvious. The value of a systematic survey lies in its ability to dissect

155

the quality of the complex attitudes held by white people and plot with some accuracy their distribution within the white population. As we have seen, our inquiry has demonstrated that the white population in the cities is not universally racist nor can it even be divided into contrasting categories that could be called racist and nonracist. White Americans are racist in degree. Some would like to keep the black man in his place, send him back to Africa if necessary. Most would not go that far but many would oppose legislation that would bring Negroes closer, especially into their neighborhoods. Some white people give verbal approval to equalitarian principles as they apply to race but they are disturbed by the pace of change in race relations which they see going on around them. Finally, there is a minority of the white population who seem to have no apparent racist orientation, who are sympathetic to the various aspects of the black protest, and in some cases contribute support to it.[1] How can all these diverse people be captured within a single national total and identified with a single descriptive term without grossly misrepresenting the extraordinary heterogeneity which we see to exist?

This having been said, it must be recognized that resistance to change in the traditional pattern of race relations, while not universal among white people, is very widespread; it is shown in one form or another by most of the white population. Some forms of change, notably the increasing racial integration in the work situation, seem to be accepted relatively easily but those that threaten to alter long-standing patterns of separation in the more private areas of life disturb many white people.

We have emphasized the fact that the central theme of conventional racist doctrine, innate racial superiority, is largely missing from contemporary white attitudes. It has been objected that interview surveys of the kind on which this conclusion is based tend to "reduce the probability of uncovering unadulterated white racism," that "because of the unfashionableness of blatantly avowed racism today" the opinion research approach "either forces or seduces many to deny their racism."[2] The implication of this objection is that white respondents present what they take to be a

---

[1]These conclusions are not unlike those reached by Robin Williams from surveys in a number of American cities in 1951, "Our general picture of the majority-group population in the communities thus far studied includes a wide range of prejudice, with true bigots at one extreme and nonprejudiced persons at the other, but with a middle range in which reside 'the gentle people of prejudice.' " Unfortunately the methods of the Williams study are not sufficiently similar to those of our study to make possible an estimate of the change in white attitudes between 1951 and 1970. See Williams, R., *Strangers Next Door.* Englewood Cliffs, N.J.: Prentice-Hall, 1964.

[2]Tollett, K.S., "Communication," *Trans-action,* March 1970, 13.

socially acceptable facade to their interviewer and cover up their "true" beliefs. This is a familiar criticism of opinion research and of course it is never possible to establish beyond question that expressed attitudes are identical with "true" attitudes, the latter being difficult to define and even more difficult to measure. An interview survey tells us what individual respondents, sitting in the security of their own home, are willing to say to a deferential middle-class woman who does not know their name and whom they never expect to see again. On the face of it this does not appear to be a very oppressive situation and one would assume that a person who felt constrained about revealing racist attitudes under these circumstances would not find many situations in which he felt more free. Fashions in belief no doubt exist, among both whites and blacks, and they effect not only expressed attitudes but true attitudes as well. Very few white people are in a position to examine the scientific literature on the genetic contribution to racial differences; they are compelled to accept external opinion of this subject whether it is authoritative, fashionable, or merely traditional. The important fact is that over the past 25 years the explanation white people give for the disadvantages they see in the black condition has moved from a genetic to a motivational one. This does not necessarily imply that they are more favorably or sympathetically disposed toward black people and their problems but it does imply far-reaching consequences for the social policies which are seen as appropriate to meet these problems.

Differences in the racial orientations of individual white people undoubtedly derive from their own lifetime experiences and from the social environment in which they now find themselves. We have not been able to trace the development of these attitudes in this study but we are able to see the influence of some of the major communities which exist within the urban white population. White people whose childhood years were spent in the South, for example, show the clear consequences of socialization within the racial mores of that region. Jewish people differ substantially from Protestants and Catholics, reflecting their own minority status and the "liberal" tradition of their culture. Lesser differences associated with national origin are also visible. These groups are not homogeneous by any means but as groups they have a different character than the general white population. However, most of those social characteristics which are not associated with these regional or ethnic divisions, that is, sex, age, income, occupation, or residence in the suburbs, show relative little relationship to racial attitudes.

The one general characteristic of the white population which is dramatically related to racial orientation is college education. The educational system our respondents passed through had relatively little effect on their attitudes regarding race if they went no further than high school graduation.

It is also evident that those men who went on to college prior to the end of World War II took away no lasting change in their racial outlook; the college women of their generation do show a change toward more positive attitudes. Yet men and women who have attended college since World War II are clearly more positive in their racial views than other white people of their own generation who have not gone to college or people of the prewar generation who did. Since the War there appears to have been a significant change in the intellectual climate of the nation's campuses on questions of race. From the fact that the racial attitudes of young white people who went no further than high school do not differ from the attitudes of older people of similar educational level we conclude that the influence of the high schools in this aspect of socialization of the nation's youth has not changed during the past 30 years. From the substantial differences in the attitudes of young college people from those of the rest of their age cohort we conclude that the college experience is contributing significantly to change in traditional white attitudes toward race in this country.

The findings of our study require us to distinguish between those elements of white attitudes which express a preference for racial separation, a denial of discriminative practices, and a resistance to change in racial patterns and the more hostile attitude toward black people which is expressed in a willingness to condone violence against them. Although many Negroes believe white people dislike them and want to keep them down, the fact is that only a small minority of the white population express overtly hostile attitudes toward Negroes. They do not hesitate to criticize black people and to show a lack of sympathy for their problems. Most of them believe the civil rights movement is pushing too fast and very few of them believe the violent aspects of the Negro protest are justified. But with all this we find very little support for counterviolence against Negroes.

That portion of the white population who do reveal this form of hostility are distinguished by their low educational level, by their lack of association with a church and by their dissatisfaction with the community which serves them. These disaffected people go beyond the negative attitudes which are not uncommon among white people into a readiness for violent answers. Although we cannot be certain of the causal direction of these relationships, it appears that in the absence of inhibitions associated with religious or educational experience grievances against the community are displaced into hostility against black people. If this presumption is correct, we should expect the proportion of hostile white people to be influenced by current political and economic conditions, with changes which increase the level of frustration and dissatisfaction also increasing the prevalence of white hostility.

The Future of White Attitudes

It cannot be doubted that since World War II there has been a massive shift in the racial attitudes of white Americans. This is demonstrated not only by the evidence of opinion polls taken during this period but also by the various acts of Congress, state legislatures, and municipalities intended to protect the civil rights of black people. This is not to say that the white population have come to a full commitment to racial equality and racial justice; the data from our surveys demonstrate how far they are from that position. But there has been a current in white attitudes, away from the traditional belief in white superiority and the associated patterns of segregation and discrimination and toward a more equalitarian view of the races and their appropriate relations. This has been a very uneven movement and many individual white people have not moved with it but the direction of the collective change has been unmistakable.

We cannot say with assurance that this movement in white attitudes will continue. Simple persistence forecasting would tell us that the trend toward racial equality and racial integration will be maintained but there are cross-currents in the present racial situation which create great uncertainty as to where the future lies.

1. The evidence from our three national surveys leaves little doubt that the perception of contact between white and black people is increasing, at work, in the schools and in public places. If we accept Homan's familiar dictum that "interaction leads to liking" we should conclude that this contact will produce more favorable attitudes toward each other among both races. Indeed our surveys show that over the 1964-1970 period an increasing proportion of whites and blacks report having friends in the other race. Unless this country experiences some basic shift in the orientation of the two races toward each other which makes it more difficult for whites and blacks to interact on a friendly basis we would expect this trend to continue.

2. We have seen that a significant upgrading of educational achievement is taking place in the younger Negro generations and there has been a growing movement of Negroes into white-collar jobs. The gap which remains is substantial, especially in occupational status, but the pace of change has accelerated in recent years and it seems most unlikely that the long-term movement of Negro families into middle-class status will be reversed. Herbert Hyman has argued that this continuing upward mobility of black people will reduce the sense of class difference felt by white people and

weaken the basis of prejudice.[3]   Citing evidence that racial prejudice is strongly influenced by differences in social class, Hyman
predicts "The apprehension about closer contact and social relations will diminish as perception of the rising education and class
position of American Negroes grows among whites." Similarly,
the recognition by increasing numbers of Negroes that their educational and occupational status is at least equal to that of the
whites with whom they associate might be expected to reduce
the tension inherent in interracial contact. Here again the long-
term trend seems to indicate a decrease in the psychological distance between the races and an increase in the opportunity for
interaction as equals.

3. The various comparisons we have been able to make of different
   segments of our white sample in the 15 cities show us that the
   most positive attitudes, on the average, are held by people with
   some college education, particularly those whose college experience
   occurred after World War II. It is by no means true that all college
   graduates hold "liberal" views of racial matters but there is strong
   evidence that the contemporary college generations are being influenced by the ethic of racial equality which has become an increasingly prominent feature of the campus culture during the last
   20 years. The colleges are pouring out successive cohorts of young
   people whose racial attitudes are in the large clearly more positive
   than those of the population into which they are moving. If we
   knew that these attitudes would in due course regress to the popular mode we would not attach any great importance to them,
   but since our evidence demonstrates that they do not, we must
   conclude that the infusion of these young people into the blood-
   stream of American society will have significant effects. As they
   move into the adult world, and eventually into positions of prestige
   and influence, their presence can hardly fail to increase the pressure
   for change away from the folkways and beliefs which have prevailed in white America for so many years.

4. We cannot consider the future of white attitudes without reference
   to black attitudes, since it is apparent that each influences the
   other. If the black people of this country were determined to separate themselves from the majority, both physically and socially,

---

[3]Hyman, Herbert H., "Social Psychology and Race Relations," in I. Katz and
Patricia Gurin (Eds.), *Race and the Social Sciences*. New York: Basic Books, 1969,15.

the trends which we have discerned in white attitudes and behavior could not continue. The act of disengagement could not fail to stimulate counteraction with all the psychological consequences which the condition of "apartheid" implies.[4]

Who can be confident that he knows which way the black population will move? In our report to the Kerner Commission we concluded that the basic motivation of the black people we interviewed in the 15 cities was toward equality rather than separation. We reported a strong impulse among black people toward "positive cultural identity" but also a general "commitment to principles of nondiscrimination and racial harmony." At that time the general orientation of the black community appeared to be integrationist and optimistic. Our report also pointed out, however, that "There is a clear trend among younger (black) people to be more separatist" in their attitudes and more willing to accept violent methods of achieving social change.

It is apparent that in the three years since our 1968 survey there has developed among some black people, on the campuses and in the inner cities, an attraction for the concept of a distinctive black culture, separate from the broader American culture. This development tends to regard integration as a form of cooptation, inclines toward nonfraternization in interracial situations, and verges into various expressions of belligerence toward white society. We cannot predict what the ultimate significance of these separatist impulses within the black community will be. They undoubtedly have influence and it may be a growing influence. Although they may represent only a small part of black opinion at the present time, one may assume that anything which tends to alienate black people from the larger American society will in due course increase their influence.

Andrew Greeley has proposed that minority ethnic groups pass through a series of predictable phases in the process of becoming acculturated and assimilated into American life.[5] As they pass beyond early stages of immigration, developing self-consciousness, and the assimilation of their elite fringe, they move into middle-class status and a stage of militancy. Greeley believes this is where the American Negro is today. Other ethnic minorities— Irish, Poles, Italians, Jews—have moved beyond this militant phase and have

---

[4]See Pettigrew's argument regarding the consequences of racial separation in Pettigrew, T. F. "Racially Separate or Together," *Journal of Social Issues, 225,* January 1969, 43-69.

[5]Greeley, Andrew M., *op. cit.,* 31.

become or are becoming fully articulated parts of the larger society. We may ask whether the black population of this country will in its turn pass beyond militancy and achieve a secure sense of American identity. Even if one takes the uncritical view that the black minority will follow the pattern of the others, it seems clear that it will not be an easy passage and it will not be achieved in this decade.

A Final Note

We close these observations regarding white attitudes with a final reminder that, despite the changes we have noted and the trends we foresee, the white population of this country is far from a general acceptance of the principle and practice of racial equality. There is little doubt that while there is collective movement of a positive character there are many white individuals whose attitudes have hardened in response to the persistent black pressure for change. These people are being confronted by demands to open their neighborhoods, integrate their labor unions, desegregate their schools, increase the black proportion of their police force, and otherwise accept changes which they consider intolerable. As we have seen, these people are found at all levels of the population and it is not likely that they will soon disappear.

We are at present at a point of uneasy confrontation. The black demands for change in the status of black people in this country are insistent and sometimes abusive. Most white people agree that change should occur but they want to move gradually and they are repelled by the violent aspects of black rhetoric and action. Change is taking place but black expectations rise as achievements rise. American society is developing a new pattern of relationships between white and black and the period of change is a time of tension for both races.

APPENDIX A

NOTES ON METHODS
IN THE 15 CITY STUDY

1. *Field Period:* Interviewing began on January 6, 1968 and ended March 31, in all places except the Cleveland suburbs. The latter extended from late March through April 30. The main race-related event that occurred from January through March was the publication of the Commission's main report at the beginning of March. Four respondents, all white and three of them suburban, mentioned the Commission's report. The assassination of Dr. Martin Luther King occurred in early April and was followed by civil disturbances in a number of cities. No disturbance occurred in Cleveland, however, and our impression is that the Cleveland suburban results were not greatly affected by these events.

2. *Sampling procedure:* All persons 16 to 69 years of age in a selected household were listed by the interviewer and the selection of respondent or respondents within the household was made objectively by the interviewer using specially prepared selection tables. These procedures, plus further weighting carried out in the course of computer analysis, produced final samples that are representative of the Negro, white, and suburban populations, respectively, as described in Note 3 below.

3. *Interviewers:* Negro respondents were interviewed by Negro interviewers and white respondents by white interviewers.

4. *The populations covered:* Each city was defined in terms of its 1960 corporate limits. The two suburban areas were defined as the towns and unincorporated areas surrounding and oriented toward Cleveland and Detroit, respectively. It is important to keep in mind certain parts of the population that were *not* included in the sample:

  a. No dormitories, military barracks, or public residential institutions (e.g., prisons) were sampled. This means, for example, that we did not sample persons who were *currently* college students or members of the armed services, except insofar as they were at that time living in private dwelling units.

  b. We did not sample persons who were living in cities but had no fixed residence, did not admit to a fixed residence, or lived in certain types of boarding houses. The main practical problem here concerns Negro males, who tend to be underrepresented by about 10 percent even in complete census counts (*Current Population Reports,* Series P-25, No. 310, 1965). In the combined 15 city sample, our ratios of males to females are .71 for Negroes and .80 for whites. Only part of this asymmetry can be due to differences in the populations (e.g., males away in the armed services, different mortality rates). Part of the problem involves locating males at all, and part involves completing interviews with those who are located and eligible.

  Since within the general population, ages 16 to 69, there is good reason to believe that the true sex ratio for Negroes is at least close to .90 and for whites well above .90 (*Current Population Reports,* Series P-25, No. 385, 1968, U.S. Bureau of the Census), we have not given total percentages based on a simple combining of males and females. In most cases we have presented results separately by sex. *Wherever we have presented totals these have been constructed by averaging the separate male and female totals.* This would seem to provide a better estimate of what a complete census enumeration would obtain than a simple combining of all cases.

  c. No matter how carefully a survey is carried out, not everyone who is eligible is actually interviewed. The two main sources of such "nonresponse" are refusals (persons unwilling to be interviewed) and "not-at-homes" (persons away from home when the interviewer calls, even with repeated callbacks). Ordinarily about 15 to 20 percent of a national target sample is missed for such reasons and it is important to determine to what extent this makes sample estimates differ from the values that would be obtained if interviews were completed with the entire target sample.

  In the present study, calculations of response rates from our 32 samples (Negro and white from each of 15 cities, plus two suburban) range from 55 to 92 percent, with a mean of 74 percent for Negroes, 68 percent for whites in cities, and 80 percent for whites in suburbs. These rates are somewhat lower than the conventionally accepted 80 to 85 percent. This is partly explicable because city response rates are, in fact, usually lower than overall national rates, and partly because the large size and narrow time limits of this survey made it impractical to reach a more desirable level.

An analysis of the Negro sample has been carried out to determine what effects nonresponse has on results presented here. This has been done by using the four cities in which Negro response rates are highest and comparing the background characteristics and attitudes of respondents interviewed on the first call, on the second call, and on subsequent calls. The results indicate moderate effects in expected directions: Those interviewed on later calls were more often males, more often employed, and more often in their 20's and 30's. Despite this difference, there seem to be no "systematic differences in attitudes between those respondents interviewed on first calls, second calls, and those interviewed on later calls" (Methodological Report No. 2, Project 45975, June 3, 1968, Survey Research Center). There are a few scattered differences, some of which are sensible in terms of the kinds of respondents missed on the first call, but there is no overall trend such that, for example, Negroes interviewed on later calls are more *or* less militant than those interviewed on the first call.

Sample Sizes by Age in Decades

	16-19	20-29	30-39	Age 40-49	50-59	60-69	Total*
Negro men	163	259	239	234	158	118	1,171
Negro women	199	408	399	314	190	133	1,643
White city men	122	232	187	199	217	185	1,143
White city women	150	299	215	287	276	212	1,439
White suburban men	20	46	26	44	31	13	180
White suburban women	23	44	39	45	24	13	188

*The age of one white city man was not ascertained.

Sample Sizes by Age and Education

	Age 16-19*	Age 20-39					Age 40-69					Total**
		8th grade or less	9-11 grades	12 grades	Some college	College graduate	8th grade or less	9-11 grades	12 grades	Some college	College graduate	
Negro men	163	51	174	169	76	28	244	117	86	47	16	1,171
Negro women	199	62	284	329	101	31	246	188	135	48	19	1,643
White city men	122	25	73	144	91	86	175	134	143	67	82	1,143
White city women	150	30	96	223	85	80	197	181	270	75	51	1,439
White suburban men	20	4	12	26	19	11	13	24	23	16	12	180
White suburban women	23	4	20	41	13	5	7	23	34	11	7	188

*This group includes all educational categories.
**The age of one white city man, the education of one white city man, the education of one Negro woman, and the education of one white city woman were not ascertained.

APPENDIX B

SAMPLING DESIGN
AND SAMPLING ERRORS

General Design of the 15-City Samples

Data reported by racial class for the 15 cities were obtained by combining individual city household samples selected to obtain about equal numbers of interviews from white and black respondents. The samples were designed to permit analyses by racial groups and comparisons between groups within each city as well as from city to city. Moderately clustered city samples of 150 to 200 interviews from each racial group were thought adequate for research purposes. To accomplish that objective required disproportionate sampling by racial classification. Although white households had equal selection probabilities within a city, black households in predominantly white blocks had a lower selection rate than black households in racially-mixed or predominantly black neighborhoods.

There were three stages of sampling. In the first stage, city blocks were sampled with probabilities proportionate to number of dwellings, after stratification by racial classification. In the second stage, an average of five dwellings was selected from each sample block. Finally, in a sample household, all persons 16 to 69 years of age were listed by the interviewer. Where only one person in the household was eligible, he or she was interviewed in half of the cases but not in the other half. Where two persons were eligible, as occurs in most households consisting of a married couple with no children over 15 years of age living at home, one was selected for interviewing. When there were three or more eligible persons in a household, at least one but not more than two were designated for the sample. The selection of respondents was made objectively by the interviewers using specifically prepared tables. The interviewers had no freedom of choice in the selection of respondents within households.

The population represented by each city sample is persons 16 through 69 years of age living in households within the 1960 corporate limits. Persons with no place of residence, the institutional population, and persons in group quarters had no chance of selection for the study.

The number of interviews with white respondents varied by city from 120 to 240 and totaled about 2,600, while about 2,800 interviews were taken with black respondents, the numbers by city ranging from 110 to 255.

The Combined Samples

Before combining the city samples to produce estimates presented in this report, the data were weighted by factors that included adjustments for disproportionate sampling of households, variable respondent selection rates within households, and differential response.

The weighting of city samples to provide a combined population has reduced the effective total sample size substantially. The reader wishing to estimate standard errors can consider the actual number of cases to be about twice their effective values. Roughly the standard error of a mean or proportion is estimated to be that obtained from a simple random sample of one-half the size of that on which the tables are based.

The Suburban Samples

In order that attitudes among city and suburban respondents might be compared, samples of the white population were selected from suburban residents around and oriented toward Cleveland and Detroit. The suburban sample designs closely approximated the city designs in that the sample households were distributed throughout the area in clusters of about five dwellings.

The Cleveland suburban sample represents the urban portion of Cuyahoga County outside Cleveland and the communities of Eastlake, Lakeline, Timberlake, Wickliffe, Willoughby and Willowick in Lake County. About 140 interviews were obtained, with a response rate of 73 percent.

The Detroit suburban area was defined to include roughly the urbanized areas of Wayne, Oakland and Macomb Counties south of Pontiac and Mount Clemens, *exclusive* of the western townships of Oakland and Wayne Counties and the southern townships of Wayne County. Approximately 200 interviews were taken and a response rate of 87 percent achieved.

The precision level of suburban estimates is equivalent to that of city estimates for one racial group. Because the two suburban samples were selected at about the same rate, the effective size of the combined samples is the sum of the two suburban samples or about 340 interviews.

General Design of National Samples

The national surveys utilize the Survey Research Center's national household sample designed to represent households in conterminous United States exclusive of those on military reservations. The 74 primary sample areas, currently located in 36 states and the District of Columbia, include 12 major metropolitan areas, 32 other Standard Metropolitan Statistical Areas (SMSA's) and 30 counties or county groups representing the less urban and the rural portions of the country. In the multistage area probability sample, first-stage stratification of SMSA's and counties is carried out independently within each of the four major geographical regions—Northeast, North Central, South, and West. Thus in a sample of 1,500 households we could expect the selections from the regions to be about 375, 410, 450, and 265.

Over all regions, the SMSA's and counties are assigned to 74 relatively homogeneous groups or strata. Twelve of the strata, containing only one primary area each, are the 12 largest metropolitan areas that are included with certainty in the national sample. The remaining 62 strata, averaging around 2,000,000 population, may contain from two to 200 or more primary areas (SMSA's or county groups) from which one is selected with probability proportionate to population. This type of sampling leads to approximately equal sample sizes from the 62 primary areas whenever self-weighting samples of households and respondents are drawn.

Instead of independent selections of 62 sample points, controlled probability selection is introduced for a more efficient sample. Within each of the four geographic regions the selections of primary areas are linked by a procedure that controls the distribution of sample areas by states and degree of urbanization beyond the controls affected through the formation of the 62 strata. This controlled selection yields a more balanced sample than would be obtained with unrestricted selection, and increases the precision of sample estimates.

As multistage area sampling progresses, within each sample point the area is divided and subdivided, in two to five stages, into successively smaller sampling units. By definition and procedure, each dwelling belongs uniquely to one sampling unit at each stage. Cities, towns and rural areas are the secondary selections; blocks or clusters of addresses in cities and towns and chunks of rural areas are the third-stage units. In the fourth stage there is a selection of small segments or clusters of dwellings where interviews are taken for a study. In the last stage of sampling, one or more respondents may be selected from among household members.

Probability selection is enforced at all stages of the sample selection; the interviewers have no freedom of choice among dwellings or among household members within sample dwellings.

The 1964, 1968 and 1970 Samples

The household samples for the 1964, 1968 and 1970 national studies were selected as described in the preceding section. Each year an objective selection of one respondent per household was made.[1] However, in 1964 and 1968, eligible respondents were citizens of voting age, while in 1970 any citizen over 17 years of age was a potential respondent. To obtain unbiased estimates, the unequal within-household selection probabilities are corrected with respondent weights which are the number of eligible persons within a household.

In each survey about 1,500 interviews were obtained, with response rates around 77 percent. In 1970 only half the white sample was asked the questions regarding race.

Measures of Sampling Variability
for Estimates from National Surveys

Sample surveys are liable to errors from several sources other than the chance occurrences of sampling. Indeed, the bias of nonresponse, errors of response (arising when misinformation is reported or questions are misinterpreted), or errors in data processing may be more serious than errors that occur because survey questions were asked of only some instead of all citizens meeting the age requirement for respondent eligibility. Nevertheless, the researcher has a responsibility to acquaint the reader with the magnitude of sampling errors of survey estimates.

In the case of probability sample designs, the type used for the national surveys reported in Chapter VI, measures of sampling variability can

---

[1] Kish, Leslie, "A Procedure for Objective Respondent Selection Within the Household, "*Journal of the American Statistical Association, 44*, 1949, 380-387.

be calculated from the sample data. Because of the multistage clustered sample design, however, the method of calculating sampling errors is considerably more complex than the formulas for simple random samples.[2] Moreover, it is impractical to calculate the sampling error for each survey statistic of which there may be hundreds or thousands. Therefore, we have prepared tables of average sampling errors, calculated by formulas appropriate to the design, for two types of estimates—percentages and the differences between percentages.

Table A gives average sampling errors associated with percentages according to the reported percentage and the size of its base (number of interviews), since the sampling error varies with those factors. The measures of sampling variability presented in the table are two standard errors. Hence, for most items the chances are 95 in 100 that the interval defined by the reported percentage plus and minus the sampling error will contain the value that would have been obtained if a complete census of eligible respondents had been taken under the survey conditions that prevailed for the sample study.

Table B presents the average sampling errors associated with differences between percentages according to the magnitudes of the percentages compared and their bases. Again, sampling errors are reported as two standard errors. In general, an observed difference as large as a particular sampling error in the table has at least 95 chances in 100 of denoting a true difference between percentages in the population rather than reflecting only the chance variations of sampling.

The measures of sampling variability presented in the tables assume that reported percentages and differences are based on all sample points. Sampling errors may be higher than those in the tables when percentages are derived from only some of the sample points (as would be the case with regional estimates) or are based on subgroups that concentrate in some sample points and occur infrequently in others (black respondents, farmers, or high income respondents, for example).

---

[2]Formulas and some details of the calculations appear in Kish, L. and Hess, Irene, *The Survey Research Center's National Sample of Dwellings.* Ann Arbor, Mich.: Institute for Social Research, The University of Michigan, 1965.

APPENDIX B – TABLE A

APPROXIMATE SAMPLING ERROR OF PERCENTAGES[a]
(in percentages)

Reported Percentages	Number of Interviews							
	1500	1000	700	500	400	300	200	100
50	3.1	3.6	4.2	4.9	5.4	6.2	7.5	10.5
30 or 70	2.8	3.3	3.8	4.5	4.9	5.7	6.9	9.6
20 or 80	2.5	2.9	3.4	3.9	4.3	4.9	6.0	8.4
10 or 90	1.8	2.2	2.5	2.9	3.2	3.7	4.5	6.3
5 or 95	1.3	1.6	1.8	2.1	2.4	2.7	3.3	4.6

[a]The figures in this table represent *two* standard errors. Hence, for most items the chances are 95 in 100 that the value being estimated lies within a range equal to the reported percentages, plus or minus the sampling error.

APPENDIX B – TABLE B

APPROXIMATE SAMPLING ERROR OF DIFFERENCES[a]
(in percentages)

Size of Subgroups	For Percentages From 35% to 65%						
	1500	1000	700	500	300	200	100
1500	4.4	4.8	5.2	5.8	6.9	8.1	11.0
1000		5.1	5.5	6.1	7.2	8.3	11.0
700			5.9	6.4	7.5	8.6	11.0
500				6.9	7.9	8.9	12.0
300					8.7	9.7	12.0
200						11.0	13.0
100							15.0
	For Percentages Around 20% and 80%						
1500	3.6	3.8	4.2	4.6	5.6	6.5	8.8
1000		4.1	4.4	4.9	5.7	6.7	8.9
700			4.8	5.2	6.0	6.9	9.0
500				5.5	6.3	7.2	9.3
300					7.0	7.8	9.7
200						8.5	10.0
100							12.0
	For Percentages Around 10% and 90%						
1500	2.6	2.9	3.2	3.5	4.2	4.9	6.6
1000		3.1	3.3	3.6	4.3	5.0	6.7
700			3.6	3.9	4.5	5.2	6.8
500				4.1	4.7	5.4	6.9
300					5.2	5.8	7.3
200						6.4	7.7
100							8.9
	For Percentages Around 5% and 95%						
1500	2.0	2.2	2.4	2.6	3.1	3.7	5.0
1000		2.3	2.5	2.7	3.2	3.8	5.0
700			2.7	2.9	3.4	3.9	5.1
500				3.1	3.6	4.0	5.2
300					3.9	4.4	5.5
200						4.8	5.8
100							6.7

[a]The values shown are the differences required for signifcance (two standard errors) in comparisons of percentages derived from two different national surveys or from two different subgroups of the same study.

APPENDIX C

INTERRELATIONS OF ITEMS IN
WHITE ATTITUDE SCALES

The racial attitudes of white people described in Chapter II were combined to form three scales, Attitude Toward Interracial Contact, Perception of Racial Discrimination, and Sympathy for the Black Protest. The interrelations of the items which were combined to form these scales are given in the following tables. The entries are Tau-betas.

Attitude Toward Interracial Contact

	Accept Negro next door	Accept Negro friend	Accept Negro playmates for children
Accept qualified Negro supervisor	.31	.22	.24
Accept Negro next door		.34	.47
Accept Negro friend			.38

Perception of Racial Discrimination

	Perceive job discrimination	Perceive housing discrimination	Believe Negro disadvantages due to discrimination
Perceive police discrimination against Negroes	.28	.18	.25
Perceive job discrimination		.38	.30
Perceive housing discrimination			.21

Sympathy with Black Protest

	Sit-ins are justified	Disturbances are protest	Disturbances not planned	Negroes not pushing too fast
Demonstrations are different from riots	.56	.15	.18	.22
Sit-ins are justified		.20	.22	.35
Disturbances are protest			.13	.15
Disturbances not planned				.19

SELECTED BIBLIOGRAPHY

"The Human Meaning of Social Change," Angus Campbell and Philip E. Converse, Eds. In preparation, to be published in 1972 by Basic Books for the Russell Sage Foundation.

Racial Attitudes in Fifteen American Cities, Angus Campbell and Howard Schuman. A Report prepared for The National Advisory Commission on Civil Disorders. Ann Arbor, Michigan: Survey Research Center, Institute for Social Research, The University of Michigan, 1968. $1 paperbound.

Elections and the Political Order, Angus Campbell, Philip E. Converse, Warren E. Miller, and Donald E. Stokes. New York: John Wiley & Sons, 1966.

Public Concepts of the Values and Costs of Higher Education, Angus Campbell and William C. Eckerman. Ann Arbor, Michigan: Survey Research Center, The Institute for Social Research, The University of Michigan, 1964. $2.50 paperbound.

The American Voter, Angus Campbell, Philip E. Converse, Warren E. Miller, and Donald E. Stokes. New York: John Wiley & Sons, 1960.

Group Differences in Attitudes and Votes, Angus Campbell and Homer C. Cooper. Ann Arbor, Michigan: Survey Research Center, Institute for Social Research, The University of Michigan, 1956. $3 paperbound.

The Voter Decides, Angus Campbell, Gerald Gurin and Warren E. Miller, Evanston, Illinois: Row, Peterson and Co., 1954.